# REVISION NOTES
# & STUDY QUESTIONS
## for Standard Grade and Intermediate
# PHYSICS

## Baillie and McCormick

D1152241

## Hodder Gibson
2A Christie Street, Paisley, PA1 1NB

# Acknowledgements

Many people have contributed to the preparation of this book. We would like to thank Rothwell Glen for his tremendous contribution as an editorial consultant. His unstinting help and advice has proved very useful at all stages of the writing process. Any mistakes and omissions are our own.

Our thanks are due also to the staff at Hodder & Stoughton, particularly Julia Morris for commissioning us and Charlotte Litt who turned a typescript into a book and clarified and helped solve many production problems.

Finally, our thanks to our families for their tolerance and forbearance for a very time consuming task. Our hope is that both students and teachers will find this book useful for these examinations.

Arthur Baillie and Andrew McCormick 1999

The publishers would like to thank Science Photo Library for the ultrasound of a human foetus on page 34.

Papers used in this book are natural, renewable and recyclable products. They are made from wood grown in sustainable forests. The logging and manufacturing processes conform to the environmental regulations of the country of origin.

Orders: please contact Bookpoint Ltd, 130 Milton Park, Abingdon, Oxon OX14 4SB. Telephone: (44) 01235 827720, Fax: (44) 01235 400454. Lines are open from 9.00–6.00, Monday to Saturday, with a 24 hour message answering service. You can also order through our website www.hodderheadline.co.uk

A catalogue record for this title is available from The British Library

ISBN 0340 73730 1

Published by Hodder Gibson, 2a Christie Street, Paisley PA1 1NB.
Tel: 0141 848 1609; Fax: 0141 889 6315; email: hoddergibson@hodder.co.uk
First published 1999
Impression number    10  9  8  7  6  5  4
Year                 2005  2004

Illustrated by Chartwell Illustrators
Typeset by Wearset, Boldon, Tyne and Wear.
Printed in Great Britain for Hodder Gibson, 2a Christie Street, Paisley, PA1 1NB, Scotland, UK by J. W. Arrowsmith Ltd, Bristol.

# Contents

# Preface

*"Problems give a good opportunity to fill out the material of the lectures and make more realistic, more complete, and more settled in the mind the ideas that have been exposed."*

Richard Feynmann, winner of the Nobel Prize for Physics in 1965, in the preface to his lectures.

This book is written for students who wish to take the examination in either Standard Grade, Intermediate 1 or Intermediate 2 Physics. It deals only with key facts and questions, so reference should be made to our accompanying text book *Standard Grade Physics* for help with any of the basic ideas.

The questions have been written to match closely all the sets of examination arrangements, and are clearly marked throughout:

Intermediate 1 level questions are denoted by

Intermediate 2 level questions are denoted by

Credit level questions are enclosed within a box, marked with a C.

General level questions are unmarked.

The longer exam-style questions at the end of each chapter put together the knowledge and understanding you have gained from each of the sections. They are similar in style to those you will be asked in the SQA examination.

The levels of the Physics Facts have been similarly marked, Credit level facts being denoted by

We hope that this book will prove useful to teachers and students in practising the skills of tackling questions prior to the examinations.

Arthur Baillie and Andrew McCormick 1999

# 1  Telecommunications and Waves

## 1.1  *Communications using waves*

**PHYSICS *facts***

- The speed of sound in air is less than the speed of light in air.
- Speed $= \dfrac{\text{distance}}{\text{time}}$, $v = \dfrac{d}{t}$
- Waves are one way of transmitting signals.
- $v = f \times \lambda = \dfrac{d}{t}$
- Frequency is the number of waves per second and is measured in Hertz.
- Wavelength is the distance covered by one wave and is measured in metres.

## QUESTIONS

1   A car driver presses the horn at the same time as the light from the car headlamp comes on.

A student who is 600 m from the car observes what happens.

a) Which signal will reach the student first, the light from the headlamp or the sound from the horn?

b) What does this tell you about the speed of light compared to the speed of sound?

2   A pair of cymbals are hit together by student A. Student B, who is some distance away, starts a stopwatch when she sees the cymbals coming together. B stops the watch at the same time that the sound reaches her. To calculate the speed of sound, what other measurement should the pupil make?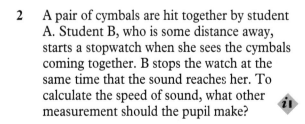

3   In an experiment to measure the speed of sound the following measurements were made.

- Time taken for the sound to reach the observer from the source = 2.4 s
- Distance from the source to the observer = 800 m

From the measurements, calculate the speed of sound.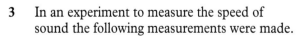

**4** Copy and complete the table.

| Speed in m/s | Distance in m | Time in s |
|---|---|---|
| a) 1500 | 1000 | |
| b) 700 | 1750 | |
| c) | 1800 | 3.4 |
| d) | 120 | 0.4 |
| e) 330 | | 7.0 |
| f) 560 | | 2.5 |

**5** During a thunderstorm a boy hears the thunder 3.5 s after he sees the lightning. The speed of sound is 340 m/s. Calculate the distance from the boy to the storm.

**6** Copy and complete the entries in the table below.

| Speed of waves in m/s | Frequency of waves in Hz | Wavelength of waves in m |
|---|---|---|
| a) | 4 | 3 |
| b) | 6 | 8 |
| c) | 0.2 | 0.15 |
| d) 12 | 3 | |
| e) 72 | 8 | |
| f) 240 | 15 | |
| g) 150 | | 0.15 |
| h) 550 | | 11 |
| i) 340 | | 17 |

**7** A wave diagram is shown below.

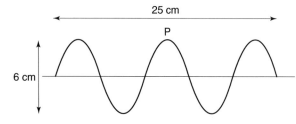

25 cm

P

6 cm

a) What is i) the amplitude, ii) the wavelength of the waves?

b) Twenty waves pass by the point P in 50 s. Calculate the frequency of the wave.

c) Calculate the speed of the waves.

**8** a) Waves of frequency 5 Hz and wavelength 0.07 m are sent across a pond. Calculate the wave speed.

b) Waves travel at a speed of 32 m/s and have a frequency of 8 Hz. Calculate the wavelength of the waves.

c) Sound waves have a speed of 350 m/s and a wavelength of 3 m. Calculate the frequency of the sound waves.

**9** Water waves travel across a harbour as shown in the diagram.

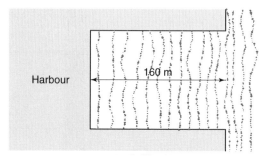

Harbour

160 m

The distance across the harbour is 160 m. The time for the waves to travel across the harbour is 20 s.

a) Calculate the speed of the waves.

b) If 40 waves travel across the harbour in this time, what is the frequency of the waves?

c) Calculate the wavelength of these waves.

**10** A wave diagram is shown below.

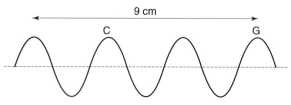

9 cm

C

G

a) What is the wavelength of the waves?

b) The crest at C takes 2 s to travel to G. Calculate the frequency of the wave.

c) What is the speed of this wave?

**11** Twenty waves pass a lighthouse in 5 minutes.

a) Calculate the frequency of the waves.

b) The speed of the waves is 6 m/s. Calculate the wavelength of the waves.

12  Middle C on a musical instrument has a frequency of 256 Hz.

a)  The speed of sound is 340 m/s. Calculate the wavelength of the note of 256 Hz.

b)  What is the time taken for this note to travel across a hall which is 60 m wide?

13  A student shouts towards a cliff which is 85 m away. The speed of sound is 340 m/s. Calculate the time from her shouting to hearing the echo.

---

**PHYSICS** *facts*

**Intermediate I only**

● If a frequency is doubled then two sounds are one octave apart.

● The frequency of a note on a stringed musical instrument can be altered by changing the length or the tightness of the string.

● In a column of vibrating air, the frequency of the sound can be increased by decreasing the length of the air column.

---

# INTERMEDIATE QUESTIONS ONLY

14  A note played on a guitar has a frequency of 256 Hz.

The string on the guitar can be altered to make a note of higher frequency. What will happen to the frequency if

a)  the length of the string is increased?

b)  the tightness of the string is increased?

c)  State the frequency of a note one octave higher.

15  A loudspeaker is placed at the top of a column of air as shown in the diagram. There is a plunger in the tube which can be moved so that the length of air in the tube can be altered. As the length of air is increased, describe what will happen to the frequency of the sound.

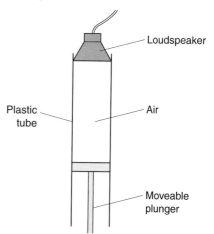

16  a)  Describe what is meant by i) a transverse wave, ii) a longitudinal wave.

b)  Give an example of each kind of wave.

## 1.2 *Communications using cables*

**PHYSICS *facts***

- Messages can be sent using a code. They are sent out by a transmitter and are replayed by a receiver.

- The telephone is an example of long range communication between transmitter and receiver.

- The energy changes that occur in a telephone are
  – sound to electrical in a microphone
  – electrical to sound in a loudspeaker.

- Electrical signals are transmitted along the communicating wires during a telephone communication.

- A telephone signal is transmitted at a speed of almost 300 000 000 m/s.

- When there is a change in the loudness of the sound, the amplitude of the sound wave changes. When there is a change in the pitch of the sound, the frequency of sound changes.

- An optical fibre is a thin glass material which is used in some telecommunication systems when the signal transmission takes place at very high speed.

- Light can be reflected from a mirror such that the angle of incidence = the angle of reflection.

- The properties of optical fibres, e.g. size, cost, weight, signal speed, signal capacity, signal quality, signal reduction per km are much better than those of electrical cables.

## QUESTIONS

1 During military conflicts, signals are often sent as code to avoid the enemy being aware of information. Describe how you might send a simple message using such a code. In your description state what apparatus you will need and how you would use it.

2 What piece of apparatus is needed a) to send out a coded message, b) to receive such a message?

3 Give the name of an instrument which can be used for long range communication between transmitter and receiver.

4 a) State the energy changes in
   i) a microphone
   ii) a loudspeaker.

   b) State where you would find both of these parts in a telephone.

5 Telephone calls take place across the world.

   a) What type of signal is sent along the wires to the exchange?

   b) How does the speed of this signal compare with the speed of sound?

**6** Use the diagram given and draw the new signal which is produced when the signal

a) doubles in frequency

b) has half the amplitude of the original signal.

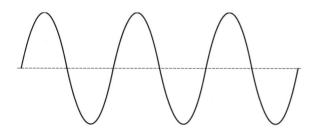

**7** Optical fibres are used to replace copper cables in many communications signals.

a) Describe what is meant by an optical fibre.

b) Describe a use of these fibres in a communications system.

c) How does the speed of the signal in the fibre compare with that in a copper cable?

**8** State two advantages of using optical fibres compared with copper cables in communication systems.

**9** The diagram shows a ray of light striking a plane mirror.

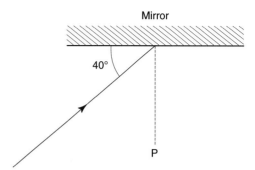

a) Copy and complete the diagram to show what happens to the ray of light as it strikes the mirror.

b) What is the name given to this effect?

c) What is the value of
i) the angle of incidence
ii) the angle of reflection?

d) What is the name given to the dotted line P?

**10** The diagram shows a ray of light in an optical fibre. Complete the diagram to show the path of a ray of light as it passes along the optical fibre.

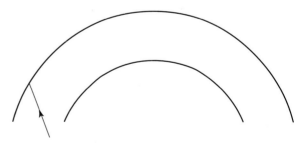

**11** Label the diagram to show the different parts of a system used to send the signal in modern communications systems. Use the terms in the list below:

optical fibre; transmitter; receiver; laser; modulator; demodulator; microphone; loudspeaker.

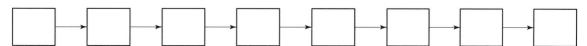

## 1.3 *Radio and television*

**PHYSICS *facts***

- Radio and television are examples of long range communication which do not need wires between transmitter and receiver.

- The main parts of a radio receiver are: aerial, tuner, decoder, amplifier, loudspeaker and electricity supply.

- The main parts of a television receiver are: aerial, tuner, decoders, amplifiers, tube, loudspeaker and electricity supply.

- A picture is produced on a TV screen due to line build-up.

- Mixing red, green and blue lights produces all the colours seen on a colour television screen.

- Radio transmission requires a transmitter. The carrier wave and audio wave are combined in a process called amplitude modulation.

- Television transmission needs transmitter, carrier wave, modulation, video and audio receivers.

- A moving picture is seen on a television screen due to: line build-up, image retention, brightness variation.

- Mixing lights with different amounts of red, green and blue produces different colours.

## QUESTIONS

**1** The following are some of the main parts of a radio receiver:

tuner; amplifier; loudspeaker.

State the missing parts in this list and explain the purpose of each missing part.

**2** One part of the radio needs to be connected to a power supply.

a) Name the part of the radio.

b) Describe why a power supply is needed.

**3** Radio transmission depends on a process called modulation. This needs a carrier wave to alter an audio wave. Complete the diagram to show the final amplitude modulated wave which is transmitted by the radio station.

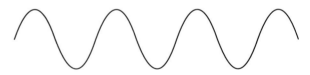

Electrical signals carrying voice information. Audio frequency

Carrier signal. Radio

4   Radios can only be used in cars if an outside aerial is connected to the car. A CD player in a car does not need an outside aerial to operate. Explain why.

5   In a television tube, electrons are accelerated from the electron gun to the end of the tube.

a) Describe how a picture is built up on the screen.

b) Explain how a moving picture is produced on the screen.

c) The brightness of the image can change on the screen. Describe what happens to cause the change in brightness.

6   a) State the three colours that are used in a television set to produce all the colours seen.

b) What colours are produced when i) red light and green light, ii) blue and green light are mixed.

## 1.4 *Transmission of radio waves*

**PHYSICS *facts***

- Mobile phones, radios and televisions are long range communication systems which do not need cables.

- Microwaves, radio and television signals are waves which transfer energy through air at a speed of 300 000 000 m/s.

- Curved reflectors on certain aerials or receivers make the received signal stronger by focusing the signals to one point.

- The period of a satellite's orbit increases as its height above the Earth increases.

- A geostationary satellite stays above the same point on the Earth's surface.

- Intercontinental telecommunication uses a geostationary satellite and ground stations.

- Satellite television uses geostationary satellites and dish aerials.

- The equation $v = f\lambda$ applies to radio waves and allows the radio station to be identified by its frequency or wavelength.

- Diffraction is the bending of waves when they pass through a narrow gap or pass over an obstacle. The amount of diffraction increases with wavelength.

## QUESTIONS

1   The table below shows the different wavebands:

| Radio waveband | Frequency range | Wavelength range | Uses |
|---|---|---|---|
| Low frequency | 30–300 kHz | 10–1 km | Long wavelength |
| Medium wave | 300 kHz–3 MHz | 1 km–100 m | Ship to shore links and radio stations |
| Short wave | 3 MHz–30 MHz | 100–10 m | Amateur radio (CB) |
| VHF | 30–300 MHz | 10 m–1 m | FM broadcasts |
| UHF | 300–3000 MHz | 1 m–10 cm | TV channels |

a)  In which waveband does BBC 1 operate?

b)  The frequency of a transmitter is 810 kHz. What type of wave does this transmitter give out?

c)  Calculate the wavelength of this transmitter.

2   a)  State one advantage of having a mobile phone.

b)  At what speed are the waves transmitted to a mobile phone?

c)  What type of wave is needed to allow this phone to operate?

3   Telephone signals are sent from Scotland to the USA. The signals are sent from a ground station to a satellite and then from the satellite to a receiving dish.

a) Why can the signals not be sent directly from Scotland to the USA, without using a satellite?

b) Explain the purpose of the satellite.

c) Why is the receiving dish curved?

---

4   A radio station is listed in a magazine as Radio 4 **LW 1500 m 200 kHz**.

a) Explain the meaning of the terms in bold.

b) Calculate the speed of the radio waves.

---

5   a) What is meant by a geostationary satellite?

b) Some satellites are in polar orbits. The period of this orbit is 2 hours. How does the height of this satellite compare with that of a geostationary satellite?

6   A curved dish is used to receive radio signals as shown in the diagram. Two signal rays come from a transmitter towards the dish aerial. Copy and complete the diagram to show how the rays reach the receiver X of the dish aerial.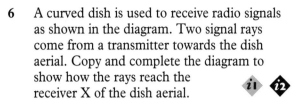

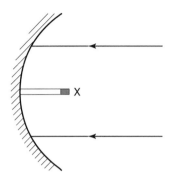

---

7   In some parts of Scotland as you pass between hills there are problems receiving certain radio stations. The frequency of the radio stations are given below.

- Station Hodder – frequency = 250 kHz
- Station Stoughton – frequency = 175 kHz
- Station Mitchell – frequency = 140 kHz

a) i) Which radio signal will bend most around the hills?
ii) Explain your answer.

b) What name is given to the effect of the bending of the radio waves round the hill?

---

## EXAM STYLE QUESTIONS

1   The space shuttle takes 90 minutes to orbit the Earth.

a) How does the height of the shuttle compare with the height of a geostationary satellite?

b) The satellite receives signals with a frequency of 4 GHz and re-transmits them at 6 GHz. (One GHz = $10^9$ Hz.) Why are two different frequencies used?

c) Calculate the wavelength of the signal with a frequency of 6 GHz.

2   A radio station is listed as 1215 kHz AM.

a) Calculate the wavelength of the signal.

b) What is meant by the term AM?

c) Explain the term modulation.

3   During the Masters golf tournament, signals are sent from America to Britain by satellite.

a) Why can these signals not be sent directly from America to Britain?

b) Explain the purpose of the satellite.

c) The distance from America to the satellite is 55 000 km. This is the same as the distance from the satellite to Britain.

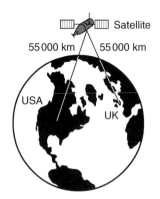

Satellite
55 000 km    55 000 km

USA
UK

Calculate the time taken for the signal to be sent directly from America to Britain.

4   Televisions consists of several different parts.

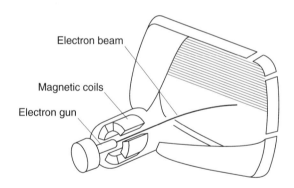

Electron beam

Magnetic coils

Electron gun

a) Explain how a picture is formed on a screen.

b) How are colours produced on the screen?

c) Moving pictures appear on screens yet we know they do not really move. How does this effect occur?

5   The Titanic ship sank on 14 April 1912 during its maiden voyage. The ship sent a radio message that it had struck an iceberg.

a) Why was radio used rather than other forms of communication?

b) At what speed do radio waves travel?

c) The radio waves were received at Halifax in Canada. The frequency of the transmitted signal was 500 kHz. Calculate the wavelength of the signal.

6   A sample of material is tested using a source of high frequency sound waves. There is a flaw in the material. The frequency of the waves is 300 kHz and the speed of sound in the material is 1500 m/s.

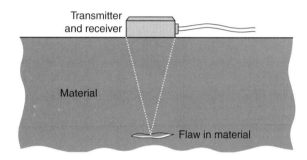

Transmitter and receiver

Material

Flaw in material

a) The signal takes $8 \times 10^{-5}$ s to be transmitted and received. Calculate the depth of the fault.

b) The fault is estimated to be at a depth of 12 wavelengths. Show by calculation whether this statement is true.

7   Sound waves are sent through liquid in a tank at a speed of 1500 m/s. The length of the tank is 600 m.

a) Calculate the time for the waves to reach the end of the tank.

b) Water waves bend as they pass around an obstacle.
i)   What is the name of this effect?
ii)   Copy and complete the diagram to show this effect.

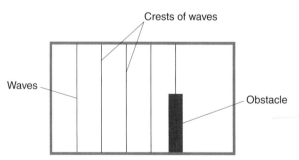

Crests of waves

Waves

Obstacle

c) The frequency of the waves is increased. Will the effect mentioned in b) increase or decrease? Explain your answer.

**8** New transmissions of TV signals will have 1200 lines on the screen compared to 625 lines at present.

a) Explain why this will give clearer pictures.

b) Explain the picture reception in terms of line build-up.

c) What must be happening inside the tube if the brightness of the screen is increased?

**9** During an event to celebrate the Millennium, reporters use a variety of methods to send their reports.

a) i) What is an advantage of using a mobile phone?
ii) By what method are the signals sent to this phone?

b) Some reporters will use a fax machine to send the details. State any advantage over a telephone message.

**10** New radio and TV stations are transmitting digital systems. To receive these signals houses need to have new aerials which are curved dishes.

a) Copy and complete the diagram to show what happens to the rays as they reach the dish.

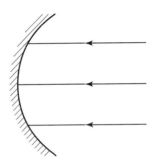

b) The dish produced by another supplier is more curved. Compare the effect of this dish on the rays with that of the dish shown in a).

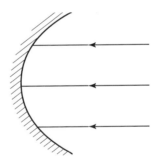

# 2 Using Electricity

## 2.1 *From the wall socket*

**PHYSICS *facts***

- Appliances with a power rating up to 700 W are normally fitted with a 3 A fuse.
- Appliances with a power rating greater than 700 W are normally fitted with a 13 A fuse.
- Fuses are intended to protect the flex of an appliance from overheating.
- Three core flexes consist of Live (brown), Neutral (blue) and Earth (green and yellow) wires.
- Two core flexes, used with double insulated appliances, consist of Live (brown) and Neutral (blue) wires.
- The Earth wire is a safety device.
- Fuses and switches are connected in the Live wire.

### QUESTIONS

1 A list of electrical appliances is shown below:

food mixer, electric fire, personal stereo, digital clock, television

Which appliance can be best matched to each of the following energy changes:
a) electrical to sound
b) electrical to light
c) electrical to heat
d) electrical to kinetic energy
e) electrical to light and sound.

2 Write down the main energy change for each of the following household appliances:
a) fluorescent lamp
b) cooker
c) washing machine
d) radio
e) kettle
f) hi-fi.

3 State an approximate power rating for each of the following household appliances:
a) hairdryer
b) kettle
c) toaster
d) light bulb.

4 Cartridge fuses of value 3 A and 13 A are available. Which value of fuse should be fitted in the 3-pin plug connected to:
a) a 1200 W vacuum cleaner?

b) a 60 W table lamp?

c) a 250 W television?

d) a 2200 W kettle?

5 The diagram shows a flex connected to a 3-pin plug.

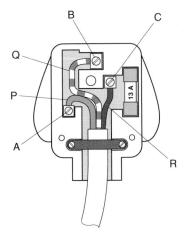

a) Name the pins A, B and C.

b) State the colours of the insulation on the wires P, Q and R.

6 A food mixer has a power rating of 140 W. The 3-pin plug attached to the flex is fitted with a 3 A fuse. The mixer develops an electrical fault which causes a current of 12 A to pass through the flex.

a) What happens to the fuse when the fault occurs?

b) What would happen if the 3-pin plug had been incorrectly fitted with a 13 A fuse?

c) What does the fuse fitted in a 3-pin plug protect? Explain your answer.

7 The table shown below gives information about four flexes.

| Flex | Power rating in W | Maximum current in A |
|------|-------------------|----------------------|
| P | Up to 700 | 3 |
| Q | 700–1380 | 6 |
| R | 1380–2300 | 10 |
| S | 2300–3000 | 13 |

Copy and complete the following table by:

a) choosing the most suitable flex for each appliance

b) stating whether a 3 A or 13 A fuse should be used in the 3-pin plug connected to the flex.

| Appliance | Power rating in W | Flex | Fuse |
|-----------|-------------------|------|------|
| i) Television | 250 | | |
| ii) Kettle | 1800 | | |
| iii) Fan heater | 2500 | | |
| iv) Table lamp | 100 | | |
| v) Vacuum cleaner | 1200 | | |

8 Most electrical appliances require to be fitted with a 3-core flex. Double insulated appliances only require to be fitted with a 2-core flex.

a) Name the wires in a 3-core flex.

b) Name the wires in a 2-core flex.

c) Draw the symbol, used on the rating plate, which indicates that an appliance is double insulated.

9 a) State the purpose of the Earth wire.

b) Explain how an Earth wire works.

10 The diagram shows part of an electric kettle.

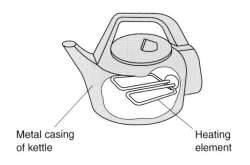

Metal casing of kettle

Heating element

a) To what part of the kettle should the Earth wire be connected?

b) Explain why the Earth wire should be connected to this part of the kettle.

11  Copy and complete the following sentences using the appropriate words from the list.

good, increased, poor, reduced

Normally the human body is a _____ conductor of electricity. However, its ability to conduct electricity is _____ when it is damp.

12  Explain the danger involving the use of an electrical appliance
a) with a frayed flex
b) with a badly connected flex
c) near a basin of water.

13  Explain why it could be dangerous to connect the 3-pin plugs of four appliances into the same wall socket using adapters.

14  The fuse in a 3-pin plug must be connected to the Live wire. Explain why this is the case.

15  To which wire, Live, Neutral or Earth, should a switch be connected? Give a reason for your answer.

# 2.2 *Alternating and direct current*

- Mains supply has a frequency of 50 Hz.

- The declared value of mains voltage is quoted as 230 V.

- The declared value of an alternating voltage is less than the peak value.

- Charge is measured in coulombs (C), current in amperes (A) and time in seconds (s).

- Charge = current × time i.e. $Q = It$

- The voltage of a supply is a measure of the energy given to the charges in a circuit.

## QUESTIONS

**1** Copy and complete the following sentences using the appropriate words from the list.

amperes, current, electrons, energy, neutrons, protons, voltage, volts

A conductor is a material in which _____ are free to move. When electrons (negative charges) move in one direction in an electrical circuit a _____ is produced. Current is measured in _____ .

The voltage of a supply is a measure of the _____ given to the charges (electrons) in an electrical circuit. Voltage is measured in _____ .

**2** Copy and complete the following sentences using the appropriate words from the list.

alternating, a.c., direct, d.c., each, one, opposite, same

When a battery is connected to an electrical circuit, electrons move in _____ direction round the circuit. Since the current only passes in _____ direction it is called _____ current (_____).

When the mains supply is connected to an electrical circuit, electrons move in one

direction, then in the _____ direction and then back again. This to and fro movement of the current is called _____ current (_____).

**3** Copy and complete the following sentences using the appropriate numbers from the list.

10, 50, 80, 115, 230

The mains supply changes direction or alternates _____ times in one second and so mains frequency is _____ Hz. The declared value of the mains supply is quoted as _____ V.

**4** Copy and complete the following sentences using the appropriate words from the list.

declared, greater, less, peak

The declared value of an alternating voltage is _____ than its peak value. Therefore, the _____ value of the mains voltage is greater than its _____ value of 230 V.

**5** Draw the circuit symbol for

a) a battery, b) a lamp, c) a switch, d) a resistor, e) a variable resistor, f) a fuse.

**6** Draw the circuit symbol for

a) a diode, b) a capacitor.

**7** Copy and complete the table.

| | Charge in C | Time in s | Current in A |
|---|---|---|---|
| a) | | 10 | 3 |
| b) | | 15 | 0.4 |
| c) | 100 | 4 | |
| d) | 1600 | 320 | |
| e) | 20 | | 0.5 |
| f) | 5 | | 0.02 |

**8** How much charge passes along a wire which carries a current of

a) 5 A for 15 s?

b) 3 A for 1 minute?

c) 0.006 A for 1 hour?

**9** There is a current of 4 A in a hairdryer when it is switched on. How much charge flows through the hairdryer when it is switched on for 3 minutes?

**10** How long does it take for a current of 2.5 A to transfer 100 C of charge through a resistor?

**11** A lamp passes 1200 C of charge in 10 minutes. What is the current in the lamp?

**12** A games console works from a 5 V supply. What does a supply voltage of 5 V mean?

**13** Describe the movement of charge in an electrical circuit when the circuit is connected to

a) a d.c. supply

b) an a.c. supply.

**14** An alternating supply has a quoted value of 16 V. Give a possible value for the peak value for this supply.

**15** What is the declared value of mains voltage?

**16** What is the frequency of the mains supply?

**17** Name the components shown below.

a)      b)

c)      d)

e)      f)

**18** Name the components shown below.

a)     b)

## 2.3 *Resistance*

- Voltage is measured in volts (V), current in amperes (A), resistance in ohms ($\Omega$) and power in watts (W).

- Voltage across a resistor = current through resistor × resistance of resistor
  i.e. **V = I R** – this is known as Ohm's Law.

- The resistance of a resistor remains constant for different currents provided the temperature of the resistor does not change.

- An ammeter is connected in series.

- A voltmeter is connected in parallel.

- Power = $\dfrac{\text{energy}}{\text{time}}$ i.e. $P = \dfrac{E}{t}$

- Power = current × voltage i.e. $P = I V$

- Power = current$^2$ × resistance i.e. $P = I^2 R$

## QUESTIONS

**1** Draw the circuit symbol for
a) an ammeter
b) a voltmeter.

**2** A pupil draws the circuit shown in the diagram below.

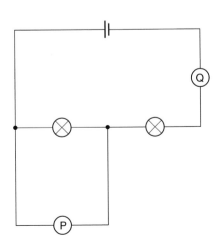

Name the type of meter labelled
a) P, b) Q.

**3** Redraw each of the diagrams given to show how *both* a voltmeter is connected to measure the voltage across component R *and* an ammeter is connected to measure the current through component S.

(a)

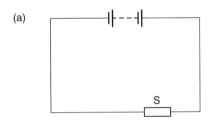

(b)

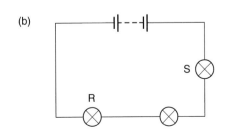

4 Copy and complete the following sentences using the appropriate words from the list.

decreases, electrical, heat, increases, joules, light, ohms, power, resistance, watts

The opposition to the flow of current is called _____ . Resistance is measured in _____ . Increasing the resistance of a circuit _____ the current in the circuit.

When a current passes through a resistor or a wire, _____ energy is changed into _____ energy.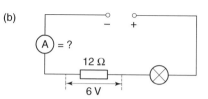

5 Copy and complete the following sentences using the appropriate word from the list. **C**

constant, decreases, increases

The equation V = I R is known as Ohm's Law. The ratio of V/I for a resistor remains approximately _____ for different currents.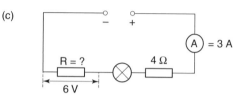

6 Name two appliances which use variable resistors.

7 Copy and complete the table shown below.

| | Voltage in V | Current in A | Resistance in Ω |
|---|---|---|---|
| a) | | 1 | 10 |
| b) | | 4 | 3 |
| c) | 5 | | 100 |
| d) | 230 | | 40 |
| e) | 0.02 | 0.01 | |
| f) | 1000 | 2.5 | |

8 Find the unknown, V, I, or R, in the circuits shown below.

(a)
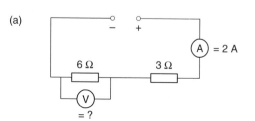

(b)
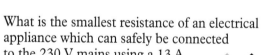

(c)

9 A current of 1.5 A passes through an 8 Ω resistor. What is the voltage across the resistor?

10 A 12 V supply is connected to a lamp. The current drawn from the supply is found to be 2 A. Calculate the resistance of the lamp.

11 A 9 V battery is connected to a 36 Ω resistor. What current passes through the resistor?

12 What is the smallest resistance of an electrical appliance which can safely be connected to the 230 V mains using a 13 A flex?

13 A lamp rated at 36 W, 3 A is connected to a 12 V supply. Calculate the resistance of the lamp when it is working at its correct rating.

14 Write down the names of three electrical appliances which change electrical energy into heat.

15 Copy and complete the following sentences using the appropriate words from the list.

divided, joules, minute, multiplied, second, watts

Energy is measured in _____ . Power is measured in _____ . Power is equal to energy _____ by time and so can also be measured in _____ in one _____ .

16 Copy and complete the table shown below.

| | Power in W | Current in A | Voltage in V |
|---|---|---|---|
| a) | | 2 | 12 |
| b) | | 0.5 | 230 |
| c) | 120 | | 60 |
| d) | 2200 | | 230 |
| e) | 0.9 | 0.1 | |
| f) | 6900 | 30 | |

17 A car headlamp is operated from a 12 V car battery. A current of 4 A passes through the headlamp when it is switched on.

a) Calculate the power rating of the headlamp.

b) How much electrical energy is used by the headlamp in 1 s?

18 Calculate the power of each of the following appliances which are connected to a 230 V mains supply.

a) The element of a kettle which has a current of 10 A passing through it.

b) The element of an electric iron which has a current of 5.5 A passing through it.

c) The element of an electric toaster which has a current of 4.0 A passing through it.

19 A shop sells two types of lamp, a filament lamp which is rated at 100 W and a discharge lamp which is rated at 25 W. Both lamps give out the same amount of light when connected to the mains supply.

a) Write down the energy change for each type of lamp and state where this energy change occurs.

b) Which lamp is more efficient at producing light?

c) How much energy does the filament lamp use in 1 s?

20 The element of an electric heater has a resistance of 50 Ω. The fire is plugged into the 230 V mains and switched on.

a) i) Write down the main energy change which takes place.
ii) State where this energy change occurs.

b) Calculate the current through the element.

c) Find the power rating of the heater.

21 A lamp is connected to an electrical supply. When the voltage across it is V volts and the current through it is I amperes, the lamp has a resistance of R ohms.

The power rating, P, of the lamp in watts is given by $P = I \times V$. Show that the power rating of the lamp can also be given by $P = I^2 \times R$.

22 Copy and complete the table shown below.

| | Power | Current | Resistance |
|---|---|---|---|
| a) | | 2 A | 15 Ω |
| b) | | $3 \times 10^{-2}$ A | 1000 Ω |
| c) | 1150 W | 5 A | |
| d) | $1.2 \times 10^6$ W | $2 \times 10^2$ A | |
| e) | 36 W | | 4 Ω |
| f) | 60 mW | | 2.4 kΩ |

23 The flex of an appliance has a resistance of 0.2 Ω. The maximum safe current that can pass through the flex is 5.0 A. What is the maximum power rating of the flex?

24 The power rating of an electric kettle is 2300 W. The element of the kettle, when switched on, passes a current of 10 A. Calculate the resistance of the element when the kettle is switched on.

25 An electric toaster has a power rating of 920 W. When operating, the element has a resistance of 57.5 Ω. Calculate the current through the element.

## 2.4 *Useful circuits*

- In a series circuit:

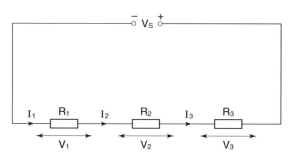

- the current is the same at all points i.e. $I_1 = I_2 = I_3$
- the supply voltage is equal to the sum of the voltages across components i.e. $V_S = V_1 + V_2 + V_3$
- the total (or combined) resistance is equal to the sum of the individual resistors i.e. $R_T = R_1 + R_2 + R_3$

- In a parallel circuit:

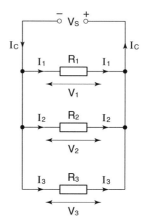

- the circuit current is equal to the sum of the currents in the branches i.e. $I_C = I_1 + I_2 + I_3$
- the voltage across components is the same i.e. $V_S = V_1 = V_2 = V_3$
- the total (or combined) resistance is given by

$$\frac{1}{R_T} = \frac{1}{R_1} + \frac{1}{R_2} + \frac{1}{R_3}$$

- In a parallel circuit, the total resistance is less than the resistance of the smallest resistor.

- An open circuit has a resistance which is so large that it cannot be measured i.e. infinite resistance (no current can pass).

- A short circuit has a very, very small resistance.

## QUESTIONS

1 For each circuit shown in the diagram below, state whether the lamps are connected in series or parallel.

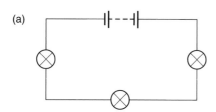

(a)

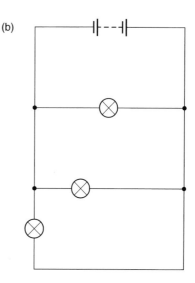

(b)

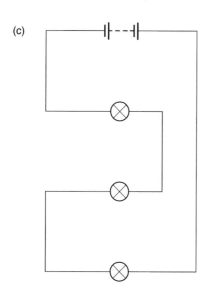

(c)

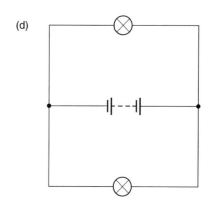

(d)

2 You are given a circuit in which the various components are all connected in series.

a) How does the current drawn from the supply compare with the current through each of the components?

b) How does the voltage of the supply compare with the voltage across each of the components?

3 You are given a circuit in which the various components are all connected in parallel.

a) How does the current drawn from the supply compare with the current through each of the components?

b) How does the voltage across the supply compare with the voltage across each of the components?

4    In the circuits shown in the diagram below,
     what are the ammeter readings
     $A_1$, $A_2$, $A_3$ and $A_4$?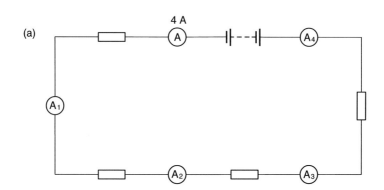

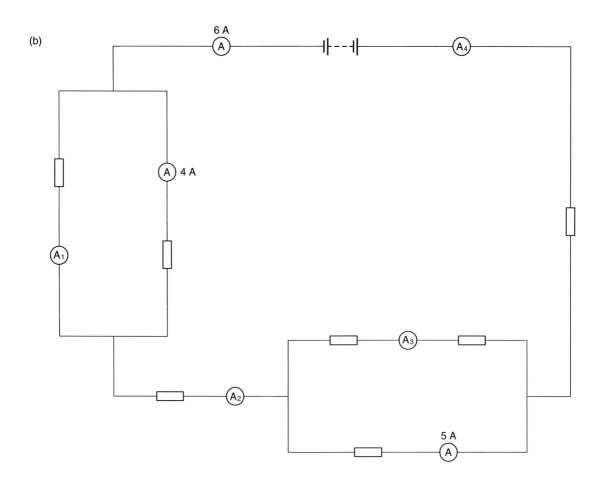

5   In the circuits shown in the diagram below, what are the voltmeter readings $V_1$, $V_2$, $V_3$ and $V_4$?  *i1* *i2*

(a)

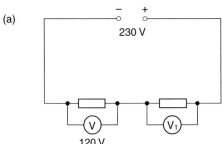

(b)

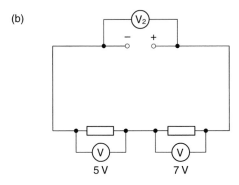

(c)

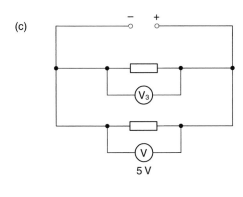

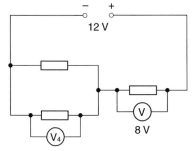

6   In the circuits shown in the diagram below, what are the missing ammeter readings $A_1$, $A_2$ and $A_3$ and voltmeter readings $V_1$, $V_2$ and $V_3$?  *i1* *i2*

(a)

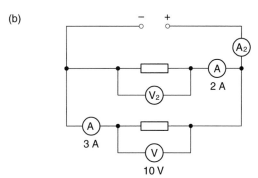

(b)

(c)

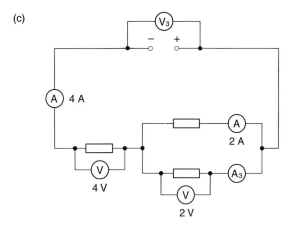

**7** Find the total resistance between X and Y in the resistor networks shown in the diagram below.

(a)
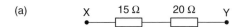

(b)
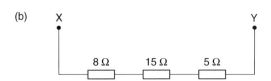

(c)
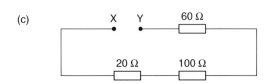

**8** Find the total resistance between X and Y in the resistor networks shown in the diagram below.

(a)
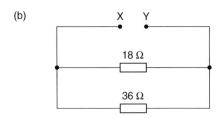

(b)

(c)
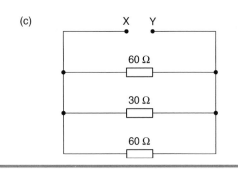

**9** Find the total resistance between X and Y in the resistor networks shown in the diagram below.

(a)
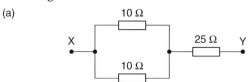

(b)
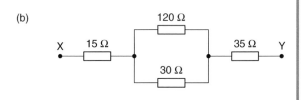

(c)
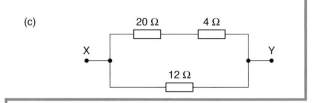

**10** An adult uses an adapter to connect a kettle, an electric fan heater and a toaster to the same mains socket. Explain why this could be dangerous.

**11** To allow a table lamp to light, two switches must be switched on, the mains switch and lamp switch.

a) Name *two* other household appliances, which require two switches to allow them to work.

b) Name any household appliance which requires three or more switches to allow it to work.

**12** A girl suspects that the fuse in the 3-pin plug attached to her stereo has blown. In order to test the fuse, she decides to make a simple continuity tester using a battery, lamp and some connecting leads.

a) Draw a circuit diagram of the circuit which could be used to test the fuse.

b) How would she know that the continuity tester was working?

c) Describe how she would use the continuity tester to test the fuse. How would she know whether the fuse was blown or not?

**13** The courtesy light of a car has to come on when either the driver's door or the passenger's door or both doors are opened. You may assume that the door switch closes when a door is opened. Draw a circuit diagram for this car courtesy light.

**14** A car has four sidelights. The sidelights can be switched on or off by a single light switch. When a lamp 'blows', the other lamps are unaffected. Draw a circuit diagram to show how the sidelights are connected to the switch and a battery.

**15** The two headlights of a car can only be switched on when the headlight switch is on and the ignition switch is on. When one headlight fails, the other headlight is unaffected. Draw a circuit diagram to show how the headlights are connected to the two switches and a battery.

**16** An ohmmeter is connected to points X and Y as shown in the diagram below.

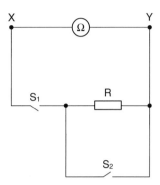

The ohmmeter reads 1000 Ω when switch $S_1$ is closed and switch $S_2$ is open.

a) The switches are altered so that $S_1$ and $S_2$ are both closed.
i) What does the ohmmeter now read?
ii) Is this an open or short circuit?

b) The switches are altered so that $S_1$ and $S_2$ are both open.
i) What does the ohmmeter now read?
ii) Is this an open or short circuit?

## 2.5 *Behind the wall*

**PHYSICS facts**

- Household wiring consists of lighting and ring circuits.

- A ring circuit is a type of parallel circuit.

- A ring circuit is designed to carry a larger current, have a larger fuse and have thicker cables than a lighting circuit.

- A ring circuit is safer than a conventional parallel circuit since each cable carries less current. This means thinner cable, which is cheaper, can be used and less heat is produced in the cables.

- Appliances are connected in parallel to the household wiring.

- Mains fuses protect the mains wiring from overheating.

- Circuit breakers, a type of automatic switch, can be used instead of fuses.

- Circuit breakers are safer than fuses since fuses can be replaced with a wrong (higher) value of fuse.

- Household electricity meters measure electrical energy in kilowatt-hours (kWh) or units.

## QUESTIONS

1  Are household appliances connected in series or in parallel to the mains supply? Give *two* reasons for your answer.

2  Why are mains fuses very important in the wiring of a house?

3  a) What is a circuit breaker?

   b) What is a circuit breaker used for?

4  Houses have two types of electrical circuit, lighting circuits and ring circuits.

   a) Describe, using a circuit diagram, a ring circuit.

   b) Give two differences between the lighting and the ring circuits.

5  The electrical meter in a house measures the number of units, or kilowatt-hours (kWh), of electrical energy used by the household. Show, by calculation, that 1 kWh = 3 600 000 J of electrical energy.

6  The consumer unit in many houses is fitted with devices which take the place of fuses.

   a) Name these devices.

   b) Give one reason why these devices are used in preference to fuses.

7  A 1 kW electric fire was switched on for 3 hours.

   a) How many kWh of electricity were used in this time?

   b) Assuming that the cost of 1 kWh is 8 p, what was the cost of the electricity used by the fire in this time?

**8** Diagrams A and B below show three identical resistors connected in parallel to a supply. The current through each resistor is 3.0 A.

b) What are the readings on the ammeters shown in diagram B?

c) Which diagram shows a ring circuit?

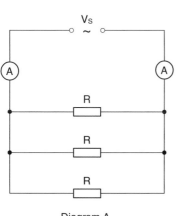

Diagram A

Diagram B

a) What are the readings on the ammeters shown in diagram A?

d) Give two reasons why diagram B is the preferred method of wiring the resistors in parallel.

# 2.6 *Movement from electricity*

**PHYSICS *facts***

- An electric motor consists of a rotating coil, a field coil (magnet), brushes and a commutator.

- A magnetic field surrounds a current-carrying wire.

- The magnetic field surrounding an electromagnet allows many electrical devices to operate e.g. an electric bell and a relay.

- A current-carrying wire experiences a force when placed in a magnetic field.

- The direction of the force on a current-carrying wire depends on the direction of the current and the magnetic field.

- A d.c. electric motor requires a commutator.

- A commutator is an automatic switch which changes the direction of the current through the rotating coil (every half revolution in a simple electric motor) and allow continuous rotation of the coil.

- Brushes are required in an electric motor to provide a good electrical connection between the commutator and the wires connected to the battery.

- Commercial motors use several coils of hundreds of turns of wire to create a greater turning effect. Each coil is connected to its own pair of commutator segments, which gives a greater turning effect and smoother running.

- Commercial motors have electromagnets instead of a permanent magnet. Electromagnets produce a stronger magnetic field than a permanent magnet of the same size.

## QUESTIONS

1   Study the electric motor shown in the diagram.

Which letter represents the
a) rotating coil?
b) field coil?
c) brushes?
d) commutator?

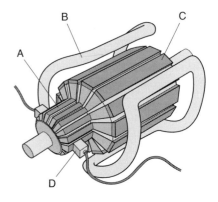

**2** Diagram A below shows the direction of four compass needles before a current-carrying wire is placed between them. Diagram B shows the effect the current-carrying wire has on the needles.

A

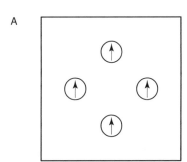

B

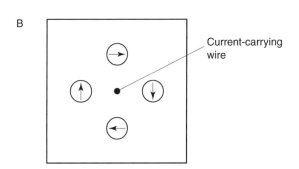

Current-carrying wire

a) Why do the compass needles move when the current-carrying wire is placed between them?

b) What would be the effect on the direction of the compass needles in Diagram B if the current through the wire
i) was switched off?
ii) was reversed?

**3** A pupil uses a power supply, a length of wire and a nail to produce an electromagnet. She does this by winding a short length of the wire 50 times round the nail and attaching the ends of the wires to a 2 V d.c. supply. She finds that the electromagnet is able to pick up five paper clips. Suggest *two* changes that would allow her electromagnet to lift more paper clips.

**4** When the switch in the diagram below is closed, the coil of wire acts as a weak electromagnet.

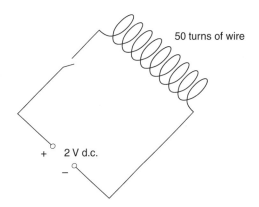

50 turns of wire

+   2 V d.c.

–

Suggest three changes to the apparatus, which would increase the strength of the electromagnet.

**5** Name *two* devices which make use of the magnetic effect of a current.

**6** A copper rod is placed across two metal tracks. The rod and tracks are placed between the poles of a large horseshoe magnet as shown below.

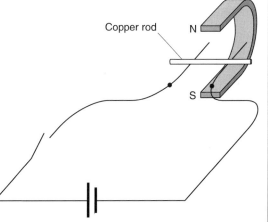

Copper rod    N

S

When the switch is closed, the copper rod moves along the tracks towards the magnet.

a) Why does the rod move along the tracks?

b) State two alternative ways of getting the copper rod to move to the left.

7  The diagram below shows a current-carrying wire that has been placed between the poles of a magnet. The wire experiences a downwards force.

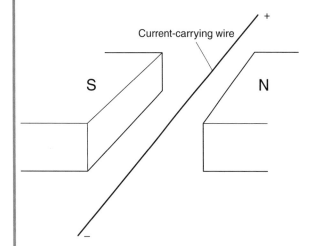

Current-carrying wire

S          N

A simple electric motor is shown below.

a)  i) State whether the coil of the motor turns clockwise or anti-clockwise.

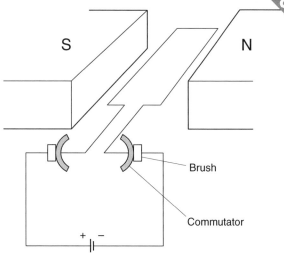

S          N

Brush

Commutator

ii) State two changes to the motor which would allow it to turn in the opposite direction.

b)  What is the purpose of the brushes?

c)  What is the purpose of the commutator?

8  Give reasons why commercial electric motors have
a)  carbon brushes
b)  multi-section commutators
c)  field coils.

## EXAM STYLE QUESTIONS

1  A replacement mains flex is to be attached to a 3-pin plug of an electric iron as shown below.

a)  Which colour of wire should be connected to each pin of the plug?

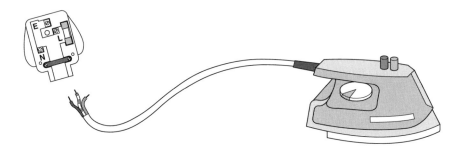

b) The rating plate of the iron is shown below.

Serial No. 57601

230 V a.c. 50 Hz

1150 to 1380 W

Calculate the maximum current passing through the flex of the iron.

c) Two of the wires from the flex are connected to the heating element and the third to the metal casing of the iron.
i) Name the two wires connected to the heating element of the iron.
ii) While the iron is being used it develops a fault which allows the Live wire to touch the casing of the iron. Describe, in sequence, what should happen when the fault occurs.

2   a) Two resistors and an ammeter are connected in series to a supply voltage of 12 V as shown below.

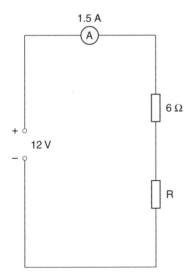

The reading on the ammeter is 1.5 A.
i) Calculate the voltage across the 6 Ω resistor.
ii) Find the value of the resistor, R.

b) Three resistors are connected as shown below.

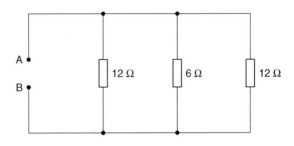

i) Calculate the resistance between A and B.
ii) A supply voltage of 12 V is now connected to A and B. Calculate the current drawn from the supply.

3   The diagram below shows the ring main circuit for the ground floor of a house. The sockets are connected to the consumer unit. The Earth wire is not shown in the diagram.

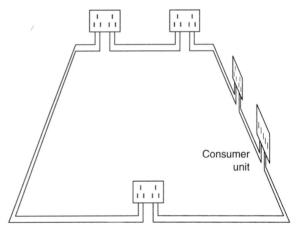

a) State one advantage of connecting the sockets in a ring circuit.

b) A 3000 W electric fire, a 270 W electric refrigerator, a 2200 W electric kettle and a 1200 W electric iron are connected to the ring main and switched on at the same time.
i) State the quoted value of mains voltage.
ii) Calculate the current drawn from the mains supply when these appliances are all switched on.

c) State one reason why a circuit breaker may be preferred to a fuse.

4  a) A diagram of a simple electric motor is shown below.

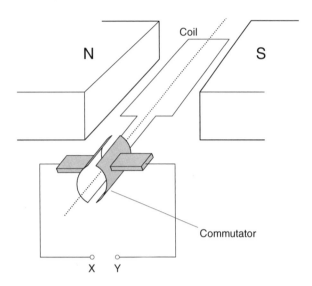

i) What must be connected between X and Y to allow the motor to rotate?

ii) Suggest two alterations which would allow this motor to turn faster.

iii) What is the purpose of the commutator?

b) The diagram below shows an electric motor from an electric drill.

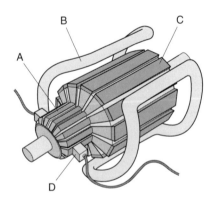

i) Name the parts of the motor marked A, B, C and D.

ii) In this motor, what is used in place of the permanent magnet shown in the simple electric motor.

5  The diagram below shows part of the wiring for the rear lights of a car. Each rear light contains two lamps. The side-lights are switched on when the front lights are switched on. The brake lights are switched on when the car brakes.

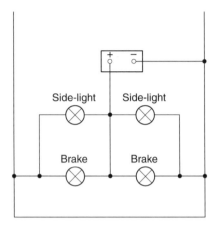

A rear side-light lamp is rated at 12 V, 6 W. A brake lamp is rated at 12 V, 24 W.

a) Explain why the lamps are connected in parallel rather than in series.

b) Calculate the resistance of
i) a rear side-light lamp
ii) a brake lamp.

c) How much current is drawn from the battery when
i) both brake lights only are on?
ii) both rear side-lights and both brake lights are on?

# 3 Health Physics and Radiations

## 3.1 *The use of thermometers*

**PHYSICS facts**

- A clinical thermometer has a smaller range than an ordinary thermometer and a kink in the tube to prevent the liquid flowing back down the tube.

- Normal body temperature is 37°C and changes in this value indicate illness.

## QUESTIONS

1 A thermometer uses liquid mercury in a glass tube to measure temperature changes. What property of the mercury makes it suitable for measuring temperature?

2 State two differences between a clinical and an ordinary thermometer.

3 Describe how you would measure body temperature using a clinical thermometer.

4 After being rescued from a mountain trip, a pupil's temperature is measured and is found to be 34°C.

a) State normal body temperature.

b) Explain why the pupil's temperature is a concern to his rescuers.

c) What is the name of the condition the climber is experiencing?

## 3.2 *Using sound*

**PHYSICS** *facts*

- The stethoscope is used as a hearing aid for doctors as it amplifies sounds within the body.

- Ultrasound is used to produce images of an unborn baby.

- Ultrasound is high frequency vibrations beyond the range of human hearing, i.e. above 20 000 Hz.

- Sound levels are measured in decibels. Above a certain noise level, sounds can be considered to be a form of pollution.

- Excessive noise can damage hearing.

## QUESTIONS

1  A stethoscope is used to detect sounds from the lungs. Explain how the closed bell is used to detect the sounds from the lungs.

2  The photo shows an ultrasound picture of an unborn baby.

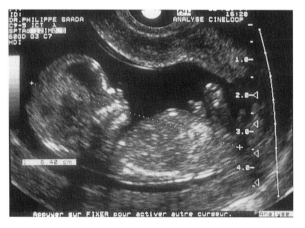

a)  Explain what is meant by ultrasound.

b)  Give another example of the use of ultrasound in medicine.

3  Ultrasound is being used to examine some tissue. The frequency of the ultrasound is 5 MHz. If the speed of ultrasound in the tissue is 1500 m/s, calculate the wavelength of the ultrasound.

4  Copy and complete the table below for the missing values when ultrasound is used to travel through tissue.

| Substance | Speed of sound in m/s | Frequency in Hz | Wavelength in m |
|---|---|---|---|
| a)  Air | 340 | 30 000 | |
| b)  Bone | 4000 | $1 \times 10^6$ | |
| c)  Tissue | 1500 | | $2 \times 10^{-3}$ |
| d)  Fat | 1450 | | $5 \times 10^{-3}$ |
| e)  Blood | | $5 \times 10^6$ | $3.2 \times 10^{-3}$ |

5  The speed of sound in blood is 1570 m/s. A blood vessel has a depth of 2.5 mm from the top to the bottom of the blood vessel. A pulsed ultrasound is reflected from the bottom of the blood vessel. Calculate the time for the ultrasound trace to be transmitted and received from the bottom of the blood vessel.

**6** An ultrasound pulse is transmitted through fat tissue. The speed of ultrasound in fat is 1450 m/s. If the wavelength used is 0.0005 m, calculate the frequency of the ultrasound pulses. **C** *i2*

**7** a) State a possible value in decibels for the sound level detected from two people having a normal conversation at a distance of 1 m.

b) What noise level will cause damage to hearing over a period of time? *i1*

**8** Pollution can be a nuisance when it occurs with sound. Give an example of sound pollution. *i1*

**9** People who mend roads often wear noise protectors when operating pneumatic drills (as in the diagram opposite). Describe how these protectors work. *i1*

HIRE

## 3.3 *Light and sight*

**PHYSICS *facts***

- Refraction is the bending of light. As a light ray goes from air to glass, it bends towards the normal.

- A convex lens converges the rays of light to a focal point but a concave lens diverges the light rays.

- The image formed on the retina of the eye is upside down and reversed.

- The focal length is the distance measured from the centre of a convex lens to the position of an image formed by a distant object.

- Power of a lens = 1/focal length in metres, and is measured in dioptres (D).

- Long sight is when distant objects can be seen clearly but objects which are close to the eye cannot. The defect can be corrected by a convex lens.

- Short sight is when near objects can be seen clearly but objects which are distant cannot. The defect can be corrected by a concave lens.

- A fibre optic source is a cold light source. This means that no heat is produced at one end of the fibre. An endoscope, an instrument used to view the inside of the body, makes use of optical fibres.

## QUESTIONS

1  Two rays of light from a distant object are shown in the diagram. The rays are shown entering the lens of a person who can see distant objects clearly.

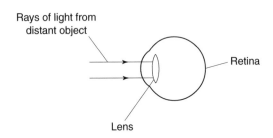

Copy and complete the diagram to show what happens to the rays as they pass through the eye to the retina.

2  Light passes from air into glass. This process is called refraction.

a) Explain what is meant by refraction.

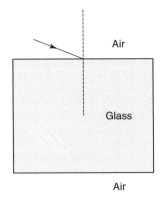

b) Copy and complete the diagram to show what happens to the ray of light as it passes from air to glass and from glass to air. Label your diagram to show the angle of incidence in the air and the angle of refraction in the glass.

3 When light passes into the eye, an image is formed on the retina. Compared to the object is the image upside down or the right way up? Explain your answer.

4 Describe how you could measure the focal length of a convex lens. In your description you should
a) state the apparatus required
b) describe how you would use the apparatus
c) state what measurement you would make.

5 The table below shows a selection of lenses of different focal lengths. Copy and complete the table to calculate the power of each lens.

| Type of lens | Focal length in cm | Power of lens in D |
|--------------|--------------------|--------------------|
| Convex | 10 | |
| Convex | 15 | |
| Convex | 25 | |
| Concave | 10 | |
| Concave | 20 | |

6 Lenses in an optician's box have the following powers
a) 15 D, b) 20 D, c) −5 D

For each lens calculate the focal length and state the type of lens.

7 Angus can see clearly objects which are close to his eyes but distant houses appear blurred.

a) What eye defect is he experiencing?

b) State the type of lens that is needed to correct this defect.

c) Copy and complete the diagram to show the effect of this lens on the rays of light entering the eye.

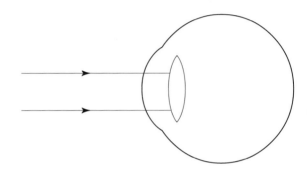

d) Sheryl needs a convex lens to correct her eye defect. State what the eye defect is.

e) Explain how this lens corrects the problem.

8 Keyhole surgery is used in several operations. This involves the use of an endoscope which has fibre optics as part of its construction.

a) What is meant by a fibre optic?

b) What is the advantage of using an endoscope as a source of light, when examining tissue inside the body?

# 3.4 & 3.5 *Using the spectrum and radiation*

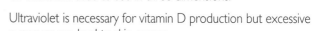

PHYSICS *facts*

- Lasers are used as scalpels, to remove tattoos and to seal blood vessels in the eye.

- X-rays are used to detect breaks in bones and digestive disorders, and are detected using photographic film.

- CT scans are used to see in three dimensions.

- Ultraviolet is necessary for vitamin D production but excessive exposure can lead to skin cancer.

- Infra red radiation is detected as heat from the human body.

- Radiation can kill living cells and can be used to treat cancer.

- Alpha radiation travels a short distance in air and is absorbed by paper; beta radiation is absorbed by aluminium; gamma radiation is reduced by lead or concrete.

- An atom has a nucleus which contains protons and neutrons surrounded by electrons.

- Ionisation is the gain or loss of an electron to make a charged particle.

- The greatest ionisation density is produced by alpha radiation.

- The radioactivity of a source is measured in becquerels (Bq) and decreases with time.

- Half-life is the time taken for a source's radioactivity to decrease to half of its initial activity.

- Dose equivalent is measured in sieverts and takes account of the type and energy of the radiation.

## QUESTIONS

1  Describe one use of lasers in medicine.

2  a) What are X-rays used for in medicine?

   b) How are X-rays detected?

3  CT scans are used to detect brain tumours. What is the advantage of this scan over a series of X-rays?

4  In some parts of the world, including the UK, there is a maximum time people should sunbathe each day.

   a) What radiation are you exposed to during sunbathing?

   b) What is the danger of excessive exposure to this radiation?

**5** Some people suffer from arthritis and this causes a rise in temperature in the joints. Which radiation will be emitted from the joint indicating the change in temperature?

**6** Radiotherapy is used to treat cancers. What does this treatment do to the cells of the tumour?

**7** Other than treatment of cancer, describe a use of radiation in medicine.

**8** There are three different types of nuclear radiation. Copy and label the diagram to show the effect of different materials on these radiations.

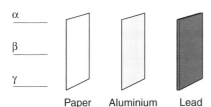

α _____

β _____

γ _____

Paper    Aluminium    Lead

**9** The atom has three particles inside it. For each statement below state the name of the particle and the charge, if any, on the particle.

| Statement | Particle | Charge |
|---|---|---|
| a) Found outside the nucleus | | |
| b) Found inside the nucleus; opposite charge to a) | | |
| c) Other particle in the nucleus | | |

**10** Nuclear radiation produces ionisation. **C**

a) What is meant by ionisation?

b) A certain nuclear radiation can easily be absorbed by paper or skin. If swallowed, however, it produces a large amount of damage. What is the name for this radiation?

**11** Photographic film is often used in radiation badge detectors. On what effect does this film depend to detect radiation?

**12** a) State the unit in which activity of a source of radiation is measured.

b) What happens to the activity of the source as time increases?

**13** a) What is meant by the half-life of a radioactive source? **C**

b) The activity of a source is measured as 10 MBq when prepared. After 24 hours it is measured as 0.625 MBq. Calculate the half-life of this source.

**14** The half-life of radon-222 is 3.8 days. The activity of a sample of radon is 50 kBq at the start of an experiment. What will be the activity in 15.2 days?

**15** Carbon-14 is used to date old samples of paper. The half-life of carbon-14 is 5730 years. A sample contains 70 mg originally, how much is left after 17 190 years?

**16** The half-life of cobalt-60 is 5.3 years. After 15.9 years, the activity is 50 kBq. What was the activity of the original sample?

**17** 100 g of gold-198 decays to 6.25 g in 10.8 days. What is the half-life of gold-198?

**18** State two safety precautions when handling radioactive sources.

**19** a) What is the unit of dose equivalent of a radioactive source?

b) What two factors does the dose equivalent take into account?

**PHYSICS** *facts*

**Intermediate 2 only**

- The absorbed dose, D, is measured in grays and is 1 J/kg.

- The quality factor, Q, is a measure of the biological effect of radiation on tissue.

- The dose equivalent, H, is equal to DQ.

## INTERMEDIATE 2 QUESTIONS ONLY

**20** What are the names of the units for measuring a) activity, b) absorbed dose and c) dose equivalent?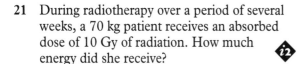

**21** During radiotherapy over a period of several weeks, a 70 kg patient receives an absorbed dose of 10 Gy of radiation. How much energy did she receive?

**22** The quality factor for gamma radiation is one. During an examination of cracks in metal, a worker is exposed to 25 µGy of gamma radiation.

  a) Explain what is meant by the quality factor.

b) Calculate the dose equivalent of this exposure.

**23** The quality factor for alpha radiation is 20, while the factor for gamma is one. During industrial testing for faults, a worker is exposed to an alpha source of absorbed dose 10 µGy and 25 µGy of gamma radiation. Calculate the total absorbed dose equivalent.

**24** State two factors which affect background radiation.

## EXAM STYLE QUESTIONS

**1** Lasers can be used to treat a wide range of conditions. Details of some lasers are given in the table below.

| Type of laser | Wavelength in nm | Power |
|---|---|---|
| Argon | 488 | 1.0 |
| Helium–Neon | 633 | 5 mW |
| Gallium arsenide | 910 | 1 mW |
| Nd YAG | 1064 | 50 W |
| Carbon dioxide | 10 600 | 15 W |
| Excimer | 193 | 20 W |

The visible spectrum goes from 400–700 nm (1 nm = $10^{-9}$ m).

a) Which laser operates in the ultra-violet range?

b) Calculate the energy given out by the carbon dioxide laser in 5 s.

c) Describe a use of lasers in medicine.

**2** A variety of lenses are used to correct eye defects.

a) Tom has difficulty seeing distant objects but can read this page clearly.
i) What eye defect is he experiencing?
ii) What kind of lens will correct this problem?

b) A lens has a power of $-3.25$ D. Calculate the focal length of this lens.

**3** Ultrasound is often used in medicine.

a) What is meant by ultrasound?

b) A lithotripter uses ultrasound to shatter kidney stones. This works at a frequency of 4 MHz.

Calculate the wavelength of this ultrasound if the speed of sound in this tissue is 1600 m/s.

c) Calculate the depth of this organ if the ultrasound can only reach 75 wavelengths.

**4** a) Sound levels can cause damage to hearing. At what value would this be likely to occur?

b) What sound level does normal conversation at 1 m have?

**5** During a building accident, people are thought to be trapped below the rubble. They can be detected using heat radiation.

a) What is the name given to this type of radiation?

b) How does the wavelength of this radiation compare with that of visible light?

c) When people go to ski in mountains, less radiation is absorbed than at lower altitudes. This means that there is more ultraviolet radiation than normal.
i) Why do we need some ultraviolet light for our bodies?
ii) What is the danger of excessive exposure to ultraviolet radiation?

**6** The diagram shows radiation passing through different materials.

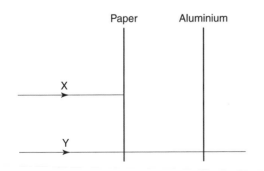

a) State the two radiations labelled X and Y.

b) One of these produces a high ionisation density.
i) What is meant by ionisation?
ii) Why is radiation X more dangerous inside the body than outside?

**7** Technetium-99m is a gamma emitter with a half-life of 6 hours.

a) Explain the terms i) gamma emitter, ii) half-life.

b) This material is combined with a drug and put into the body to go to a specific organ such as the kidneys. The gamma radiation is detected by a gamma camera. Why is a gamma emitter used?

c) To treat a tumour with radiation, the radiation is directed at different directions around the body as shown in the diagram. Explain why this method is used.

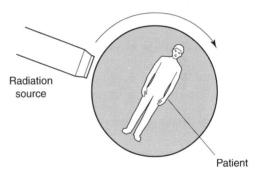

**8** A student injures a leg during a sports event. At the hospital an X-ray is taken of the leg.

a) Explain whether a break in the bone will show as a black or a white line.

b) To ensure that there are no further problems a CT scan is taken of the leg.
i) What is the advantage of this scan?
ii) The scan requires 20 'slices' to be taken and each slice will be 8 mm thick. What is the total length exposed to radiation?

c) After the plaster is removed some weeks later, infrared radiation is shone onto the skin to help the fracture in the final healing. How will the patient detect this radiation?

# 4 Electronics

## 4.1 *Overview*

**PHYSICS *facts***

- All electronic systems can be broken down into three parts – input, process and output.
- An analogue signal has a continuous range of values.
- A digital signal has two possible values. The signal is either at a maximum value, called a HIGH or logic '1', or at a minimum value, called a LOW or logic '0'.

## QUESTIONS

**1** Electronic systems consist of three parts. Name these parts.

**2** The output signals from four devices are each displayed in turn on an oscilloscope screen as shown below.

(a)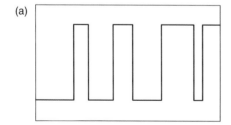

(b)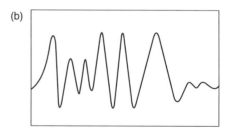

(c)

(d)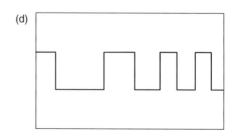

Which of these signals can be classified as digital and which as analogue?

**3** What is the difference between a digital signal and an analogue signal?

## 4.2 *Output devices*

**PHYSICS *facts***

- An output device changes electrical energy into some other form of energy.

- Examples of output devices are a loudspeaker, an electric motor, a relay, a solenoid, a lamp, a light emitting diode (LED) and a 7-segment display.

- The relay, solenoid, LED and 7-segment display are all digital output devices.

- The loudspeaker, electric motor and lamp can be analogue or digital output devices – when the output device is either on or off then the device is digital but if the output signal to the output device varies in value then it is analogue.

- LEDs will only light up when connected to the power supply the correct way round.

- A resistor should always be connected in series with an LED – this protects the LED from damage from too high a current passing through it (or too high a voltage across it).

- Decimal numbers may be converted into binary numbers e.g. decimal 7 in binary is 0 1 1 1 and decimal 9 in binary 1 0 0 1.

## QUESTIONS

1   Name two digital output devices and state the energy conversion for each one. *i1* *i2*

2   Name two analogue output devices and state the energy conversion for each one. *i1* *i2*

3   Draw the circuit symbol for a light emitting diode (LED). *i2*

4   A girl connects an LED, a resistor and a 9 V battery in series. The LED lights. The girl then makes three changes to the circuit, *each change following in turn from the last*:

Change P – she reverses the connections of the LED, *then*

Change Q – she reverses the connections of the battery, *then*

Change R – she connects the LED to the battery by removing the resistor.

What is the effect on the LED of the changes P, then Q and then R?

5   The diagram below shows an electrical circuit.

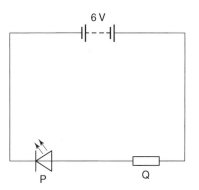

a)  Name components P and Q?

b)  Explain why component Q is necessary in the circuit.

**6** The diagram below shows a 7-segment display.

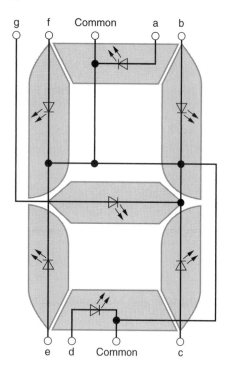

List the number or numbers which can be displayed on a 7-segment display when the LED in segment e is not working?

**7** The following is a list of output devices.

lamp, buzzer, solenoid, relay, LED, motor

Which output device could be used to

a) operate the central locking mechanism of a car?

b) move a conveyor belt?

c) alert a car driver that a door is open?

d) indicate that a microwave programme is complete?

**8** A student is asked to design a suitable circuit to light an LED. The components available are a 9 V battery, a switch, an LED and a resistor.

a) Draw a suitable diagram, which will allow the LED to light when the switch is closed.

b) The maximum voltage across the LED must not exceed 1.8 V and the maximum current must not exceed 12 mA.

Calculate the value of the resistor required for the circuit.

**9** Calculate the decimal equivalent of the binary numbers

a) 0 0 1 0, b) 1 0 0 0, c) 0 1 1 1, d) 1 0 0 1

## 4.3 *Input devices*

**PHYSICS** *facts*

- Examples of input devices are microphones, thermocouples, solar cells, thermistors, light dependent resistors (LDR), capacitors, potentiometers, switches.

- The resistance of a thermistor changes with temperature.

- The resistance of an LDR decreases with increasing light level.

- An uncharged capacitor has no voltage across it.

- As a capacitor charges up, the voltage across the capacitor increases with time until it reaches the same value as the supply voltage.

- The time taken to charge a capacitor depends on the values of the capacitor and the series resistor – increasing the value of the capacitor increases the time taken or increasing the value of the series resistor increases the time taken.

- For the following circuit

$$\frac{V_1}{V_2} = \frac{R_1}{R_2}$$

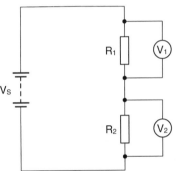

## QUESTIONS

1 What is the energy conversion for
a) a microphone?
b) a thermocouple?
c) a solar cell?

2 A number of input devices are shown in the list below.

microphone, thermocouple, solar cell, thermistor, light dependent resistor (LDR), capacitor

From this list, choose an appropriate input device which could form part of a circuit to be used for the following:

a) a timer circuit for a microwave oven

b) to charge batteries during the day

c) to adjust the brightness of a television to suit the light level in the room

d) to measure the temperature of a Bunsen flame

e) to allow a sound to be observed on an oscilloscope.

**3** A student measures the resistance of a thermistor using an ohmmeter. The reading on the ohmmeter is 10 000 Ω when the thermistor is on the bench.

What happens to the reading on the ohmmeter when the student places the thermistor

a) nearer the window where the light intensity is greater but the temperature is the same?

b) close to a warm radiator where the light intensity is unchanged?

**4** A student measures the resistance of a light dependent resistor (LDR) using an ohmmeter. When the LDR is on the bench the reading on the ohmmeter is 2000 Ω.

The student now moves the LDR to the window where the light intensity is greater. What happens to the reading on the ohmmeter?

**5** A student carries out an experiment to see how the resistance of an LDR changes with light intensity and obtains the results shown in the table below.

| Light intensity in units | Voltage across LDR in V | Current through LDR in A |
|---|---|---|
| 100 | 5 | 0.0025 |
| 200 | 5 | 0.0045 |
| 300 | 5 | 0.0070 |

a) Calculate the resistance of the LDR at each of these light intensities.

b) How does the resistance of the LDR depend on light intensity?

c) Draw a circuit diagram of the apparatus the student could have used to obtain these results.

**6** A student uses the apparatus shown below to measure the resistance of a thermistor. When the temperature of the thermistor is 20°C, the reading on the voltmeter is 6 V and the reading on the ammeter is 0.12 A.

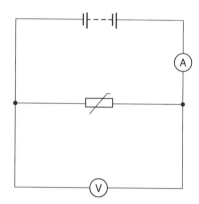

a) Calculate the resistance of the thermistor at this temperature.

b) The resistance of the thermistor is found to decrease as the temperature increases. Suggest suitable readings on the ammeter and voltmeter when the thermistor is at a temperature of 15°C.

7   A student uses the circuit shown below to investigate the charging of a capacitor.

When the switch is open the reading on the voltmeter is zero.

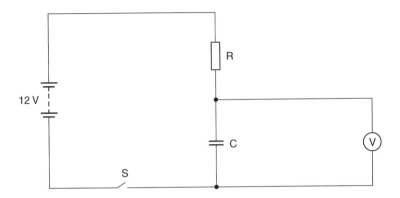

a) When the switch is closed, what happens to the reading on the voltmeter?

b) The student has two capacitors of values 1 μF and 10 μF and two resistors of value 10 kΩ and 100 kΩ. Which combination of capacitor and resistor in the circuit shown would give
i)   the shortest time to charge the capacitor?
ii)  the longest time to charge the capacitor?

8   Name an appropriate input device which could be used as part of a circuit for the following:
a)  an electronic thermometer
b)  an electronic egg timer
c)  a decibel meter (to measure noise level)
d)  an electronic light meter.

9   The diagram below shows two resistors connected to a 9 V battery.

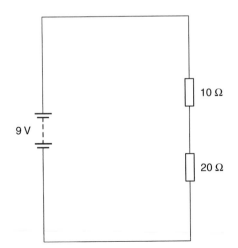

a)  What is the total resistance of the circuit?

b)  Calculate the current drawn from the battery.

c)  Find the voltage across i) the 10 Ω and ii) the 20 Ω resistors.

**10**  In the following circuits shown below find the voltages $V_1$ and $V_2$.

(a)

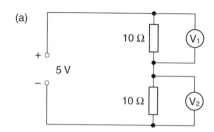

(b)

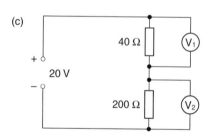

(c)

**11**  In the following circuits shown below find the voltage $V_2$ and the resistance $R_2$.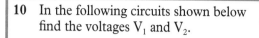

(a)

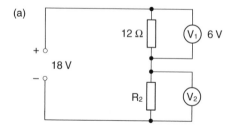

(b)

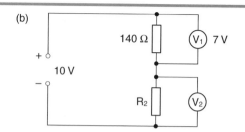

(c)

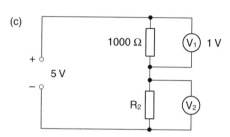

(c)

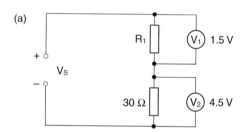

**12**  In the following circuits shown below find the resistance $R_1$ and the supply voltage $V_S$.

(a)

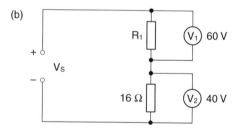

(b)

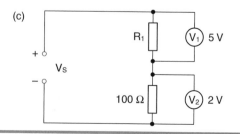

## 4.4 *Digital processes*

- A transistor is an electrically-operated switch. The circuit symbol for an NPN transistor is

- A transistor is off (non-conducting) for voltages below a certain value (normally below 0.7 V) but on (conducting) at voltages at or above this certain value (at or above 0.7 V).

- Logic gates are digital devices – NOT (or Inverter), AND and OR gates.

- Logic gates use logic '1' to represent a high voltage level (HIGH) and logic '0' to represent a low voltage level (LOW).

- A truth table shows how the output from a gate or system varies with the input or inputs.

- The circuit symbols and truth tables for NOT, AND and OR gates are

| Input | Output |
|-------|--------|
| 0 | 1 |
| 1 | 0 |

| Input A | B | Output |
|---------|---|--------|
| 0 | 0 | 0 |
| 0 | 1 | 0 |
| 1 | 0 | 0 |
| 1 | 1 | 1 |

| Input A | B | Output |
|---------|---|--------|
| 0 | 0 | 0 |
| 0 | 1 | 1 |
| 1 | 0 | 1 |
| 1 | 1 | 1 |

- A timing circuit or oscillator can be built from a resistor, capacitor and a NOT gate (Inverter) to give clock pulses

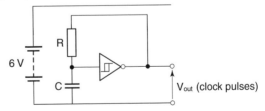

- The clock pulses can be more frequent (frequency increased) by decreasing the value of the capacitor or the value of the resistor.

- The clock pulses (zeros and ones) are digital and can be counted using a counter circuit.

- The output of a counter is in binary and this can be changed into a decimal number using a binary to decimal circuit.

## QUESTIONS

**1** The diagram below shows an electronic circuit.

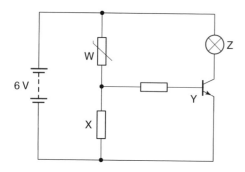

a) Name the components W, X, Y and Z in the circuit.

b) What is the purpose of component Y in the circuit?

**2** A student builds the electronic circuit shown below.

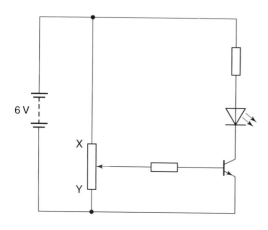

The LED is lit when the potentiometer is at position X.

a) When the LED is lit, is the transistor on (conducting) or off (non-conducting)?

b) The slider on the potentiometer is slowly moved from X to Y. What happens? Is the transistor now on or off?

**3** The diagram below shows a transistor switching circuit.

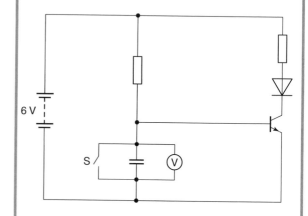

Switch S is closed.

a) i) State the reading on the voltmeter.
ii) Is the transistor on (conducting) or off (non-conducting)?
iii) Is the LED lit or unlit?

b) Switch S is now opened. Explain what happens in the circuit.

**4** Study each of the circuits shown below. In circuit (b) the resistance of the thermistor decreases as its temperature increases.

(a)

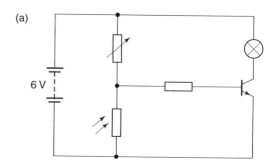

(b)

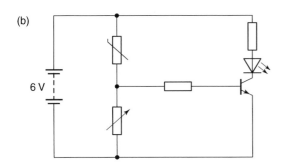

(c)

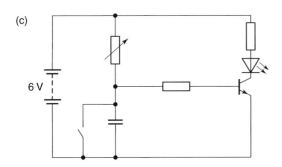

i) Suggest one possible practical use for each of these circuits.

ii) Why is a variable resistor used in each of these circuits instead of a fixed resistor?

**5** The diagram (right) shows a circuit built by a student for a greenhouse. The resistance of the thermistor decreases as its temperature increases.

a) Explain what will happen as the temperature in the greenhouse increases.

b) The student now uses the same components to build a circuit which will sound the buzzer when the greenhouse gets too cold.

Draw a suitable circuit diagram.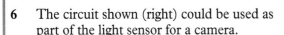

**6** The circuit shown (right) could be used as part of the light sensor for a camera.

Explain what happens when the camera goes from a brightly lit room to a dimly lit room?

**7** Draw the circuit symbol for an NPN transistor.

**8** a) Draw the circuit symbol for a NOT gate.

b) Write down the truth table for a NOT gate.

c) State an alternative name for a NOT gate.

**9** a) Draw the circuit symbol for an AND gate.

b) Write down the truth table for an AND gate.

**10** a) Draw the circuit symbol for an OR gate.

b) Write down the truth table for an OR gate.

**11** Why is a truth table important?

**12** When using logic gates, the terms high voltage (HIGH) and low voltage (LOW) are used.

Which of these terms correspond to logic '1' and which to logic '0'.

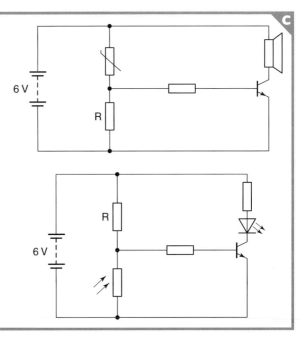

**13** A student makes up the truth tables shown below for three different logic gates. Name each of the logic gates identified by the truth table shown below.

A

| Input | | Output |
|---|---|---|
| **A** | **B** | |
| 0 | 0 | 0 |
| 0 | 1 | 1 |
| 1 | 0 | 1 |
| 1 | 1 | 1 |

B

| Input | Output |
|---|---|
| 0 | 1 |
| 1 | 0 |

C

| Input | | Output |
|---|---|---|
| **A** | **B** | |
| 0 | 0 | 0 |
| 0 | 1 | 0 |
| 1 | 0 | 0 |
| 1 | 1 | 1 |

**14** Copy and complete the truth table for the circuit shown below.

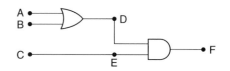

| A | B | C | D |
|---|---|---|---|
| 0 | 0 | | |
| 0 | 1 | | |
| 1 | 0 | | |
| 1 | 1 | | |

**15** Copy and complete the truth table for the circuit below.

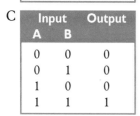

| A | B | C | D | E | F |
|---|---|---|---|---|---|
| 0 | 0 | 0 | | | |
| 0 | 0 | 1 | | | |
| 0 | 1 | 0 | | | |
| 0 | 1 | 1 | | | |
| 1 | 0 | 0 | | | |
| 1 | 0 | 1 | | | |
| 1 | 1 | 0 | | | |
| 1 | 1 | 1 | | | |

**16** A student is asked to design a circuit to switch on a lamp when it is dark and a master switch is switched on.

- The light sensor gives logic '1' when in light.
- The master switch gives logic '1' when closed.
- The lamp is switched on by logic '1'.

Draw a suitable logic diagram, naming the logic gates used.

**17** The buzzer of a house alarm sounds when the alarm panel is switched on and either the light sensor is broken or the pressure pad is stood on.

- The alarm panel gives logic '1' when switched on.
- The light sensor gives logic '1' when in light.
- The pressure pad gives logic '1' when stood on.
- The buzzer is switched on by logic '1'.

Draw a suitable logic diagram, naming the logic gates used.

**18** The circuit diagram for a clock pulse generator is shown below.

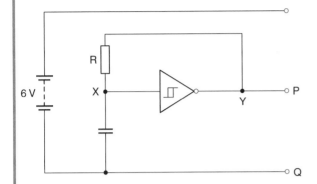

a) When the circuit is switched on the capacitor is initially uncharged.
i) What is the voltage across the capacitor at this time?
ii) State the logic levels at X and Y when the capacitor is uncharged.
iii) What is the voltage across the resistor when the capacitor is uncharged?

b) The capacitor begins to charge up.
i) What happens to the voltage across the capacitor?
ii) What will eventually happen to the logic levels at X and Y?

c) The capacitor now begins to discharge.
i) What now happens to the voltage across the capacitor?
ii) What eventually happens to the logic levels at X and Y?
iii) What happens now?

**19** The diagram shown in Question 18 is part of an electronic oscillator circuit.

a) A suitably adjusted oscilloscope is connected across PQ. Sketch the trace obtained on the screen.

b) What name is given to the pattern on the oscilloscope screen?

c) Explain how this electronic oscillator circuit works.

d) The circuit can be altered to give more oscillations per second.

Suggest *two* ways of obtaining a higher frequency from this circuit.

**20** a) What name is given to an electronic circuit which can count pulses from a clock pulse generator?

b) Name a practical device which contains such a circuit.

**21** The output from a counter circuit consists of logic '1's and logic '0's only, which is difficult for most humans to understand.

a) What name is given to the output of logic '1's and logic '0's from a counter circuit?

b) The output from a counter circuit is usually fed into a circuit which changes the logic '1's and logic '0's into a form that we can easily understand. What name is given to this form of counting?

## 4.5 *Analogue processes*

- An amplifier is an analogue process device which makes electrical signals larger.

- Audio amplifiers are found in devices such as radios, televisions, hi-fi's, intercoms and loud hailers.

- The output signal from an audio amplifier has the same frequency as, but a larger amplitude than, the input signal.

- For an amplifier:

  $$\text{Voltage gain} = \frac{\text{output voltage}}{\text{input voltage}} \text{ and}$$

  $$\text{Power gain} = \frac{\text{output power}}{\text{input power}}$$

- Power, $P = IV = I^2 R = \dfrac{V^2}{R}$

## QUESTIONS

1   A number of electrical devices are listed below

baby alarm, electric cooker, hi-fi, microwave, radio, television, vacuum cleaner, washing machine

From the above list write down the names of the devices in which amplifiers play an important part.

| | Voltage gain | Input voltage | Output voltage |
|---|---|---|---|
| a) | | 0.01 V | 5.0 V |
| b) | | 5 mV | 3.0 V |
| c) | 750 | 0.02 V | |
| d) | $3 \times 10^4$ | 1.5 mV | |
| e) | 150 | | 6.0 V |
| f) | $4.8 \times 10^5$ | | 12.0 V |

2   a) An amplifier is a major component in an intercom. What is the purpose of the amplifier in this device?

b) How do the frequencies of the input and output signals of an amplifier compare?

c) How do the amplitudes of the input and output signals of an amplifier compare?

3   Copy and complete the table for an amplifier.

4   The input voltage to an amplifier is 0.12 V and the output voltage from it is 18.0 V. Calculate the voltage gain of this amplifier.

5   The voltage gain of an amplifier is 500. Calculate the voltage at the output of the amplifier when the voltage at its input is 0.03 V.

6   An amplifier has an output voltage of 6.0 V. The voltage gain of the amplifier is 100 000. What is the input voltage to the amplifier?

7 A student is asked to measure the voltage gain of an amplifier. Describe, with the aid of a circuit diagram, how the student measures the voltage gain of the amplifier shown below.

```
┌─────────────────────────────────┐
│                                 │
│          Amplifier              │
│                                 │
│     ○              ○            │
│                                 │
│    Input          Output        │
│                                 │
│     ○              ○            │
│                                 │
└─────────────────────────────────┘
```

8 Copy and complete the table shown below for an amplifier.

| | Power gain | Power input | Power output |
|---|---|---|---|
| a) | | 0.16 W | 8.0 W |
| b) | | $3.0 \times 10^{-5}$ W | 18 mW |
| c) | 20 | 0.04 W | |
| d) | 1500 | 4.5 μW | |
| e) | 700 | | 4.2 W |
| f) | 5000 | | 0.03 W |

9 The power output of an amplifier is 30 W when the power input to it is 0.02 W. What is the power gain of the amplifier?

10 The input power to an amplifier is 5 mW. Calculate the output power of the amplifier when it has a power gain of 5000.

11 An amplifier has a power gain of $2 \times 10^6$ and an output power of 5 W. What is the input power to the amplifier?

12 Copy and complete the table shown below.

| | Power in W | Voltage in V | Resistance in Ω |
|---|---|---|---|
| a) | | 5 | 100 |
| b) | | 12 | 20 |
| c) | 50 | 2 | |
| d) | 1000 | 230 | |
| e) | 36 | | 0.25 |
| f) | 40 | | 2.5 |

13 A microphone having a resistance (impedance) of 75 kΩ is connected to the input terminals of an amplifier. The microphone produces a steady voltage of 3 mV.

Calculate the power output of the microphone.

14 An amplifier provides a power output of 9.6 J of energy every second to a loudspeaker. The loudspeaker has a resistance (impedance) of 15 Ω.

a) What is the power output of the amplifier?

b) Calculate the voltage across the loudspeaker.

15 A circuit provides $1.6 \times 10^{-8}$ W to the input terminals of an amplifier. The input voltage to the amplifier is 20 mV.

a) Calculate the resistance (impedance) of the circuit.

b) The power output of the amplifier is 15 W. Find the power gain of the amplifier.

## EXAM STYLE QUESTIONS

**1** a) A pupil writes down a list of electronic components. The list is shown below.

microphone, switch, loudspeaker, light emitting diode (LED), light dependent resistor (LDR), thermistor, capacitor, motor

i) Construct a table with suitable headings which show the components correctly listed as input devices or output devices.
ii) What energy change takes place in a microphone?

b) An electronic circuit is shown below.

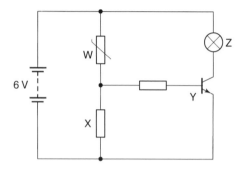

i) Name components W, X, Y and Z.
ii) Suggest a use for this circuit.

**2** a) A light dependent resistor (LDR) is connected in series with a 3 kΩ resistor and a 12 V supply as shown below.

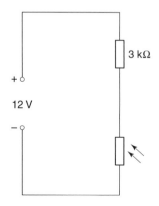

At a particular light level during the day, the voltage across the LDR is 4 V.
i) What is the voltage across the resistor?
ii) Calculate the resistance of the LDR.

b) A graph of resistance of the LDR against light intensity is shown below.

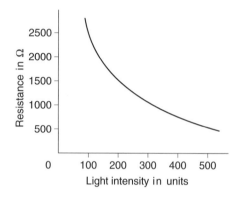

Use the graph to estimate the light intensity falling on the LDR.

c) The circuit shown below is fitted in a car. The circuit is designed to alert the driver when it has become too dark for the car to be driven safely without the car lights being switched on.

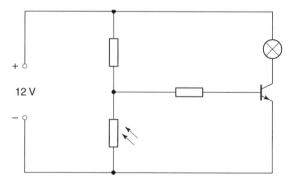

Describe how the circuit works.

3    Some types of portable electrical equipment
     can be damaged by connecting the battery the
     wrong way round. The circuit shown below
     indicates whether the 9.0 V battery is correctly
     connected between P and Q.

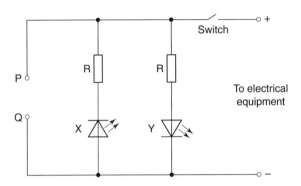

     The LEDs are identical and normally operate
     at 1.8 V and 8 mA.

     a)  Which LED, X or Y, would light when the
     9.0 V battery was connected the correct way
     round?

     b)  Calculate the value of the series resistor, R,
     required to allow the LED to operate
     normally.

4    The logic diagram for the operation of a car
     interior light is shown below. The interior
     lamp will come on when either door is open
     provided the lamp switch is on.

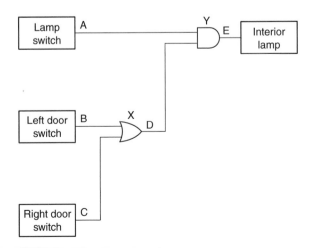

- The lamp switch gives logic '1' when it is switched on and logic '0' when switched off.

- Either door switch gives logic '1' when a door is opened and logic '0' when a door is closed.

- The lamp lights with logic '1'.

a) Name i) logic gate X and ii) logic gate Y.

b) Copy and complete the truth table for the system when the lamp switch is on.

| A | B | C | D | E |
|---|---|---|---|---|
| 1 | 0 | 0 | | |
| 1 | 0 | 1 | | |
| 1 | 1 | 0 | | |
| 1 | 1 | 1 | | |

5   A pupil is asked to measure the voltage gain of an amplifier. The pupil sets up the circuit shown below.

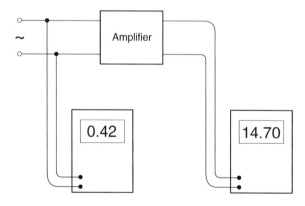

a) The multimeters, connected to the circuit to measure the input and output voltages, can be set to measure d.c. current, a.c. current, d.c. voltage, a.c. voltage and resistance.

Which of these quantities should the multimeter be set to measure?

b) Calculate the voltage gain of the amplifier.

c) The input signal has a frequency of 500 Hz. What is the frequency of the output signal?

# 5 Transport

## 5.1 *On the move*

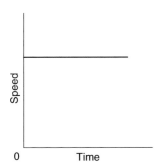

(a) Constant speed

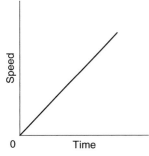

(b) Constant acceleration

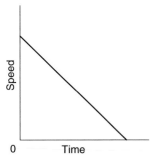

(c) Constant deceleration

- Distance is measured in metres (m), time in seconds (s) and average speed in metres per second (m/s).

- Average speed = $\dfrac{\text{total distance travelled}}{\text{total time taken}}$

- Instantaneous speed is approximately equal to the average speed provided the time used is very small.

- Speed is the distance travelled by an object in a time e.g. a speed of 5 m/s means the object will travel 5 metres in 1 second.

- Acceleration is the change in speed of an object in one second e.g. an acceleration of 2 m/s² means that the body will increase its speed by 2 m/s every second.

- Change in speed is measured in metres per second (m/s), time for change in speed to occur is measured in seconds (s) and acceleration is measured in metres per second squared (m/s²).

- Acceleration $= \dfrac{\text{change in speed}}{\text{time for change in speed to occur}}$

  $= \dfrac{\text{final speed} - \text{initial speed}}{\text{time for change in speed to occur}}$

- $a = \dfrac{v - u}{t}$

- The speed–time graphs (left) show: a) constant speed, b) constant acceleration and c) constant deceleration.

- The distance travelled by an object is equal to the area under a speed–time graph.

- For an object moving with constant acceleration (or constant deceleration) then

  average speed $= \dfrac{\text{initial speed} + \text{final speed}}{2} = \dfrac{u + v}{2}$

## QUESTIONS

1   You are about to make a journey in a car. You wish to measure the average speed of your journey.

Describe how you would measure the average speed of your journey.

2   Copy and complete the table shown below.

|   | Average speed | Distance | Time |
|---|---|---|---|
| a) |  | 50 m | 5 s |
| b) |  | 1000 m | 200 s |
| c) | 4 m/s | 80 m |  |
| d) | 20 m/s | 1 km |  |
| e) | 6 m/s |  | 15 s |
| f) | 100 m/s |  | 120 s |

3   A girl on a bicycle travelled a distance of 500 m in 125 s. What was her average speed?

4   Between two bus stops, a bus travels at an average speed of 10 m/s. It took 150 s to travel between the stops. How far apart were the bus stops?

5   During a 100 m sprint, a boy's average speed was calculated to be 8 m/s. How long did the boy take to complete the sprint?

6   A lorry travelled a distance of 15 km in 10 minutes. Calculate the average speed of the lorry in metres per second.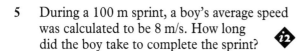

7   A train covered a distance of 150 km at an average speed of 40 m/s. Calculate the time taken by the train to cover this distance.

8   A snail travelling at an average speed of 0.2 cm/s, took half a minute to cross a leaf. Calculate the distance covered by the snail in this time.

9   Describe how you could measure the instantaneous speed of a bicycle at a certain time in its journey.

10   What is the difference between average speed and instantaneous speed?

Give two examples of situations where average and instantaneous speeds are different.

11   Explain the meaning of the terms a) speed, b) acceleration.

12   What is meant by a speed of a) 3 m/s, b) 10 cm/s, c) 150 km/h

13   What is meant by an acceleration of a) $2\ \text{m/s}^2$, b) $10\ \text{m/s}^2$, c) $-4\ \text{m/s}^2$

14   Copy and complete the table shown below.

| | Acceleration in m/s² | Change in speed in m/s | Time for change in s |
|---|---|---|---|
| a) |  | 20 | 5 |
| b) |  | 5 | 10 |
| c) | 2 |  | 8 |
| d) | 0.5 |  | 20 |
| e) | 3 | 12 |  |
| f) | 2.5 | 37.5 |  |

15   The speed of a car increased by 20 miles per hour in 5 seconds. Calculate the acceleration of the car in miles per hour per second.

**16** Copy and complete the table shown below.

| Acceleration in m/s² | Initial speed in m/s | Final speed in m/s | Time for change in s |
|---|---|---|---|
| a) | | 0 | 10 | 5 |
| b) | | 3 | 13 | 10 |
| c) | | 2 | 34 | 8 |
| d) | | 5 | 0 | 5 |
| e) | 3 | 4 | | 4 |
| f) | 6 | 2 | 20 | |
| g) | −3 | | 6 | 7 |
| h) | −4 | 12 | | 4 |

**17** A bus started from rest and had a constant acceleration of 1.5 m/s². What was the speed of the bus
a) 3 s, b) 5 s, c) 10 s after starting?

**18** A plane accelerates uniformly from rest to 36 m/s in 20 s. What was the acceleration of the plane?

**19** A train travelling at 15 m/s accelerated uniformly to 35 m/s in 120 s. Calculate the acceleration of the train.

**20** A small boat travelling at 10 m/s decelerated uniformly to rest in 25 s. Calculate its
a) change in speed, b) deceleration.

**21** A vehicle accelerated uniformly at 3 m/s². What time did it take for the speed to increase from 4 m/s to 16 m/s?

**22** A car accelerated uniformly from rest to 60 miles per hour in 12 s. Calculate the acceleration of the car in miles per hour per second.

**23** Draw a speed–time graph to show the motion of a vehicle travelling at a constant speed of 5 m/s for 6 s.

**24** A bus accelerated uniformly from rest to 10 m/s in 5 s. It then travelled at this speed for a further 4 s. The bus then decelerated uniformly for 6 s to 4 m/s. Draw a speed–time graph for the motion of the bus.

**25** Describe the motions represented by the speed–time graphs shown below.

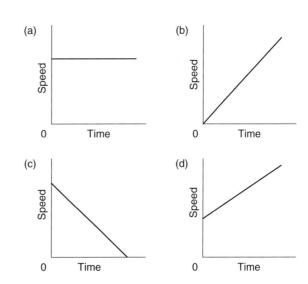

**26** The speed–time graphs for different objects are shown below. Calculate the acceleration of each object.

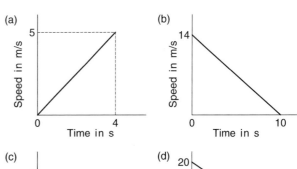

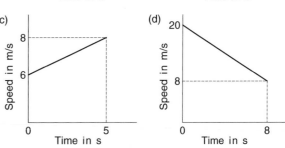

# 5 Transport

**27** Find the distance travelled and the accelerations of the objects whose speed–time graphs are shown below.

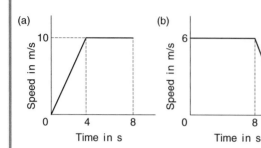

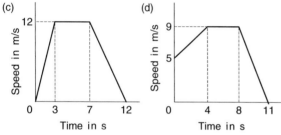

**28** The speed–time graph for a ball dropped onto the floor and rebounding is shown below.

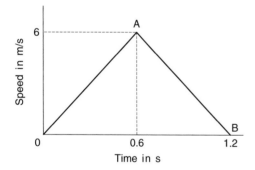

a) Describe the motion of the ball between i) OA and ii) AB.

b) Calculate the acceleration of the ball between i) OA and ii) AB.

c) Calculate the distance travelled by the ball.

d) What was the initial height of the ball above the floor?

**29** The speed–time graph for a vehicle is shown below. C

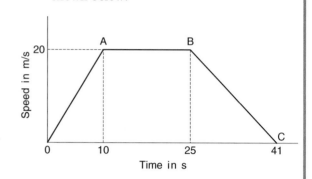

a) Describe the motion of the vehicle between i) OA, ii) AB and iii) BC.

b) Calculate the acceleration of the vehicle between i) OA, ii) AB and iii) BC.

c) Calculate the distance travelled by the vehicle.

d) Calculate the average speed of the vehicle.

**30** A trolley accelerated down a slope. A student suggested two methods to measure the instantaneous speed of the trolley at point X.

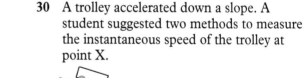
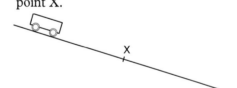

Method A – the student used a stopwatch to time how long the length of the trolley took to pass point X on the slope.

Method B – the student uses a light gate and timer to time how long the length of the trolley took to pass point X on the slope.

a) Explain why each method is liable to give a different instantaneous speed for the trolley at point X.

b) Which method is likely to give the best estimate of the instantaneous speed at point X?

## $5.2$ *Forces at work*

**PHYSICS** *facts*

- A force or a number of forces acting on an object can change its speed, its direction of travel and/or its shape.

- A newton balance is used to measure the size of a force.

- Force is measured in newtons (N).

- The force of friction usually opposes the direction of travel of an object.

- It can be advantageous to increase the force of friction when you do not wish something to start moving or when you wish something that is moving to slow down e.g. car brakes.

- It can be advantageous to reduce the force of friction when you wish something to move more easily.

- Equal forces acting in opposite directions on an object are called balanced forces.

- When balanced forces or no forces act on an object, the object either remains at rest or continues to move at constant speed – this is Newton's First Law of motion.

- Mass is measured in kilograms (kg), acceleration in metres per second squared (m/s$^2$) and force in newtons (N).

- $F = m\,a$ – this is often called Newton's Second Law.

- Mass is measured in kilograms (kg), weight in newtons (N) and gravitational field strength in newtons per kilogram (N/kg).

- Mass is the quantity of matter (solid, liquid or gas) forming an object. The mass of an object remains constant wherever it is taken e.g. a 10 kg mass on Earth is still a 10 kg mass in outer space.

- Weight is a force and is due to the pull of the Earth on an object.

- The weight per unit mass (i.e. weight/mass) is called the gravitational field strength.

## QUESTIONS

1  Describe three effects that a force can have on an object.

2  Describe how you would use a newton balance to measure the force applied to an object.

**3** Copy and complete the following sentences using the appropriate words from the list.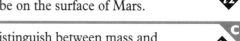

Earth, force, gravitational, newtons, weight

The force of gravity or _____ is a force and so is measured in _____ . Weight is due to the pull of the _____ on a body. The weight per unit mass is called the _____ field strength and for the Earth its value is 10 N/kg.

**4** Copy and complete the table shown below.

| | Weight in N | Mass in kg | Gravitational field strength in N/kg |
|---|---|---|---|
| a) | | 2 | 10 |
| b) | | 5.4 | 10 |
| c) | 35 | | 10 |
| d) | 5 | | 10 |
| e) | 120 | 12 | |
| f) | 40 | 4 | |

**5** What is the weight of a 5 kg mass on the Earth?

**6** An object was placed on a newton balance. What was mass of the object when the reading on the balance was 6 N?

**7** An astronaut has a mass of 60 kg on Earth. She lands on the moon where the gravitational field strength is 1.6 N/kg.

a) What is the astronaut's weight on the Earth?

b) What is the astronaut's mass on the moon?

c) Calculate the astronaut's weight on the moon.

**8** A space probe of mass 300 kg lands on Mars where the gravitational field strength is 3.8 N/kg. Calculate the weight of the probe on the surface of Mars.

**9** Distinguish between mass and weight.

**10** A car is travelling due North. In which direction does

a) the engine force act?

b) the force of friction act?

**11** There are many everyday situations where it is useful to

a) increase the force of friction

b) decrease the force of friction.

For a) and b) describe *two* of these situations.

**12** Copy and complete the following sentences using the appropriate words from the list.

balanced, constant, no, opposite, same, unbalanced

When equal forces act on an object in _____ directions, then they are balanced and are equivalent to _____ force at all. When no force or a system of _____ forces act on an object then its speed remains _____ .

**13** State Newton's First Law.

**14** A car is travelling at constant speed. The engine force and force of friction are the only forces acting on the car. Draw a labelled diagram showing the forces acting on the car. Indicate on your diagram the direction of travel.

**15** A lampshade of mass 1.2 kg is suspended from the ceiling by a flex.

a) Calculate the weight of the lampshade.

b) What is the value of the tension in the flex and in what direction does it act? Explain your answer.

**16** For each of the following objects, explain the motion of the object in terms of the forces acting on it:

a) a parachutist moving towards the ground at constant speed

b) a clock which is at rest on a table

c) a cyclist travelling along a level road at constant speed.

**17** Explain, in terms of the horizontal force or forces acting on a person, why seat belts are used in cars and buses.

**18** For the objects shown below calculate the unbalanced force acting on each one.

(a)

2 N        6 N

(b)

7 N        3 N

(c)
14 N        14 N

(d)
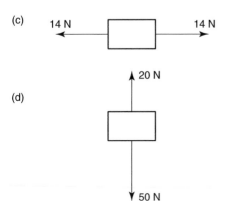
20 N

50 N

**19** Copy and complete the table shown below.

| | Unbalanced force in N | Mass in kg | Acceleration in m/s² |
|---|---|---|---|
| a) | | 5 | 3 |
| b) | | 0.7 | 2 |
| c) | 6 | 18 | |
| d) | 100 | 4 | |
| e) | 6 | | 0.2 |
| f) | 300 | | 50 |

**20** Calculate the unbalanced force required to accelerate a 1500 kg car at 2 m/s².

**21** A braking force of $6.6 \times 10^4$ N was applied to a lorry of mass 44 tonnes (1 tonne = 1000 kg). Calculate the deceleration of the lorry.

**22** An unbalanced force of 96 kN acted on a train which accelerated at 1.2 m/s². Calculate the mass of the train.

**23** Copy and complete the table shown below.

| | Force applied in N | Frictional force in N | Mass in kg | Acceleration in m/s² |
|---|---|---|---|---|
| a) | 10 | 2 | 4 | |
| b) | 4 | 1 | | 2 |
| c) | 6 | | 9 | 0.5 |
| d) | | 3 | 4 | 2 |

**24** A 0.5 kg trolley accelerated at 3 m/s² when a force of 2 N was applied to it.

a) Calculate the unbalanced force acting on the trolley.

b) Find the value of the frictional force acting on the trolley.

**25** During take off, the engine of an aircraft provided a constant thrust. The aircraft had a mass of 1200 kg and accelerated at 2.7 m/s². A constant frictional force of 500 N acted on the aircraft during the take off.

a) Calculate the unbalanced force on the aircraft during the take off.

b) Calculate the thrust of the engine.

**26** During the flight of a rocket

a) the mass of the rocket decreased as fuel was used up

b) there was a reduction in the engine thrust as booster engines stopped firing.

Describe the effect each of these changes had on the acceleration of the rocket.

## 5.3 *Movement means energy*

**PHYSICS** *facts*

- Force is measured in newtons (N), distance in metres (m) and work done in joules (J).

- Work done = force × distance

- The work done in lifting an object through a vertical height is equal to the gain in gravitational potential energy.

- Mass is measured in kilograms (kg), gravitational field strength in newtons per kilogram (N/kg), vertical height in metres (m) and potential energy in joules (J).

- Gravitational potential energy, $E_p = m\,g\,h$

- The work done in increasing the speed of an object is equal to the gain in kinetic energy.

- Mass is measured in kilograms (kg), speed in metres per second (m/s) and kinetic energy in joules (J).

- Kinetic energy, $E_k = \frac{1}{2}mv^2$

- Energy can be changed from one form to another i.e. the amount of energy does not change – this is known as the Conservation of Energy.

- Work done is measured in joules (J), time in seconds (s) and power in watts (W).

- Equations that can be used for power are

$$\text{Power} = \frac{\text{energy transferred}}{\text{time}}$$

$$\text{Power} = \frac{\text{work done}}{\text{time}}$$

$$\text{Power} = \frac{\text{gain in gravitational potential energy}}{\text{time}}$$

$$\text{Power} = \frac{\text{gain in kinetic energy}}{\text{time}}$$

## QUESTIONS

1   A car, which uses petrol as a fuel, is travelling along a straight, horizontal road. Describe the main energy change which takes place when the car
a) accelerates
b) moves at constant speed
c) brakes.

2   A petrol engined car is travelling along a straight road. Describe the main energy change which takes place when the car travels at constant speed
a) up a slope
b) down a slope.

3   Copy and complete the following sentences using the appropriate words from the list.

greater, gravitational, gravity, kinetic, smaller, work

When energy is transferred, _____ is done. When work is done against or by the force of _____, then there is a change in _____ potential energy. When the speed of an object changes then the work done on the object has caused a change in _____ energy. The _____ the mass and/or the speed of the moving object the greater the kinetic energy.

4   Copy and complete the table shown below.

|     | Work done in J | Force in N | Distance in m |
|-----|-----|-----|-----|
| a)  |     | 5   | 2   |
| b)  | 50  | 2   |     |
| c)  | 3000 |    | 60  |
| d)  |     | 300 | 0.5 |
| e)  | 5   | 15  |     |
| f)  | 100 |     | 0.4 |

5   A box is pulled 3 m along the floor by a horizontal force of 50 N. Calculate the work done on the box.

6   A boy used 3000 J of energy when pedalling his bicycle 40 m along a horizontal road. What force did the boy exert on the bicycle?

7   During braking, a car loses 45 000 J of energy. The braking force is 1500 N. Calculate the distance the car travelled during braking.

8   The engine of a train exerts a force of 8 kN and does $2 \times 10^6$ J of work. How far did the train travel?

9   A 100 kg filing cabinet is pushed 25 cm so that it is against a wall. During this movement 60 J of work are done. Calculate the horizontal force the person exerted on the cabinet.

10  A 1500 kg car travelled 0.5 km along a horizontal road at constant speed. The engine exerted a force of 3000 N.

a) State the size of the frictional force which acts on the car.

b) Calculate the work done against friction

11  Copy and complete the table shown below.

|     | Power in W | Work done in J | Time in s |
|-----|-----|-----|-----|
| a)  |     | 500 | 5   |
| b)  | 10  |     | 300 |
| c)  | 25  | 1000 |    |
| d)  |     | 10  | 50  |
| e)  | 100 |     | 120 |
| f)  | 0.5 | 100 |     |

12  A blender does 4.2 kJ of work in 30 s. Calculate the power of the blender.

13  How much work is done by a 12 W electric motor in 2 minutes?

**14** What time does it take for a 0.96 kW machine to convert 4800 J of energy?

**15** Copy and complete the table shown below.

| | Kinetic energy in J | Mass in kg | Speed in m/s |
|---|---|---|---|
| a) | | 2 | 2 |
| b) | 40 | | 4 |
| c) | 62.5 | 5 | |
| d) | | 10 | 8 |
| e) | 1000 | | 5 |
| f) | 0.9 | 20 | |

**16** A girl on roller blades is moving at a speed of 1.5 m/s. The total mass of the girl and roller blades is 40 kg. How much kinetic energy does the girl have?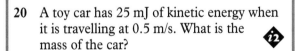

**17** A football travelling at 5 m/s has 27 J of kinetic energy. What is the mass of the football?

**18** A 0.2 kg linear air track vehicle has 0.4 J of kinetic energy. Calculate the speed of the vehicle.

**19** A 50 g ball bearing is propelled across a floor at a speed of 20 cm/s. Calculate the kinetic energy of the ball bearing.

**20** A toy car has 25 mJ of kinetic energy when it is travelling at 0.5 m/s. What is the mass of the car?

**21** A 1500 kg car has 675 kJ of kinetic energy. Calculate the speed of the car.

**22** Copy and complete the table shown below.

| | Gravitational potential energy | Mass | Vertical height |
|---|---|---|---|
| a) | | 3 kg | 2 m |
| b) | 180 J | 20 kg | |
| c) | 100 J | | 4 m |
| d) | | 200 g | 2 m |
| e) | 6 J | 100 g | |
| f) | 10 J | | 50 cm |

**23** How much gravitational potential energy does a 5 kg package gain when lifted 1.5 m?

**24** A 4 kg bag is lifted onto a shelf and gains 72 J of gravitational potential energy. Calculate the vertical height the bag was lifted.

**25** A brick drops 3.6 m onto the ground and loses 90 J of gravitational potential energy. Find the mass of the brick.

**26** A 25 kg sack is pulled 4 m along a level floor by a horizontal force of 100 N. The sack is then lifted 0.8 m onto a work bench. Calculate the total work done on the sack.

27 A 1.5 kg ball is dropped from a window
5 m onto the ground below. The effects
of air resistance may be ignored.

a) Calculate the loss in gravitational
potential energy of the ball.

b) What is the kinetic energy of the ball just
before it hits the ground?

c) Find the speed of the ball just
before it hits the ground.

28 A 45 kg swimmer steps off a diving board
and falls, from rest, into the water. The
swimmer is travelling at 8 m/s just before she
hits the water. The effect of air resistance
may be ignored.

a) Calculate her kinetic energy just before
hitting the water.

b) What is her gravitational potential energy
just as she steps off the diving board?

c) Find the height of the diving board
above the water.

29 A crane lifts a 250 kg bucket through a
vertical height of 20 m to the top of a
building in 30 s. Calculate

a) the gravitational potential energy
gained by the bucket

b) the minimum power output of the
crane.

30 A lift travels 35 m vertically up a lift shaft at
constant speed in a time of 50 s. The lift has
a total mass of 5000 kg.

a) Calculate the gravitational potential
energy gained by the lift.

b) What is the minimum power output
of the lift motor?

## 5.4 *Mechanics and heat – kinematics*

**PHYSICS** *facts*

The following Physics Facts and questions are for those taking Intermediate 2 Physics. See also Physics Facts for Chapter 5 Section 1

- A scalar quantity has magnitude (size) only e.g. 10 m; 5 s; 2 m/s.

- Examples of scalar quantities are distance, speed, time and energy.

- A vector quantity has magnitude (size) and direction e.g. 10 m East; 2 m/s North.

- Examples of vector quantities are displacement, velocity, momentum acceleration.

- Displacement is the distance travelled together with the direction.

- Velocity = $\dfrac{\text{displacement}}{\text{time}}$ $\qquad v = \dfrac{s}{t}$

- Acceleration = $\dfrac{\text{change in velocity}}{\text{time}}$ $\qquad a = \dfrac{v - u}{t}$

- A resultant force is a single force which can replace a number of forces acting on a body.

- Momentum = mass × velocity

- In all collisions, total momentum before = total momentum after.

## INTERMEDIATE 2 QUESTIONS ONLY

**1** What is the difference between distance and displacement?

**2** What is the difference between speed and velocity?

**3** a) Describe the difference between a scalar quantity and a vector quantity.

b) Name two scalar and two vector quantities.

**4** A fork lift truck has the following motions

- constant acceleration of 0.5 m/s² from rest for 4 s, then

- constant velocity for 6 s, then

- decelerates to rest in 5 s, then

- remains at rest for 1 s, then

- reverses at 0.4 m/s² for 2 s, then

- comes to rest in a further 4 s.

Draw a velocity–time graph for the fork lift truck.

5  A ball is dropped vertically from a window of a house onto the ground below. Part of the vertical velocity against time graph for the ball is shown below.

6  A 35 kg student is standing on a 20 kg trolley which is at rest. He jumps off the trolley giving a kick which sends it off at 3.8 m/s. What is the speed of the student?

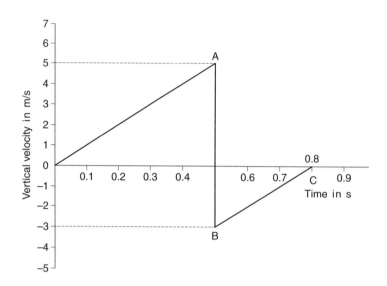

a) Describe the motion of the ball during i) OA, ii) BC.

b) Calculate the height of the ball above the ground before it was dropped.

c) To what height does the ball rebound?

d) At what time does the ball hit the ground? Justify your answer.

7  An ice hockey player of mass 62 kg is travelling at 3.5 m/s. He collides with another stationary player whose mass is 53 kg. Both players lock together to prevent them falling. What is their combined velocity?

8  A truck of mass 1200 kg is travelling at 15 m/s when it collides with a stationary car of mass 800 kg. Both the truck and the car lock together. Find their combined velocity.

## EXAM STYLE QUESTIONS

1  a) Lynne cycles to and from school. Her journey takes her along a straight road, passed her friend Susan's house. Susan decides to measure Lynne's average speed as she passes her house. She uses a stopwatch and a measuring tape.

Describe how Susan could measure Lynne's average speed as she travels past her house.

b) During a part of her journey, Lynne has to carry her bicycle up a flight of stairs. There are 10 stairs, each stair being 8 cm high. Her bicycle has a mass of 15 kg.
i) What is the minimum force required to lift the bicycle?
ii) Calculate the work done in raising the bicycle up the flight of 10 steps.

**2** a) A ship of mass 240 000 kg was towed at a constant speed of 1.5 m/s by a tug. The tug exerted a force of 1200 N on the towing cable when pulling the ship.

What is the size of the resistive force of the water opposing the motion of the ship?

b) The towing cable was then released and the ship decelerated to rest. The resistive force of the water on the ship remained constant as the ship came to rest.

i) Calculate the deceleration of the ship.
ii) How long did it take for the ship to come to rest after the towing cable was released?
iii) Draw a graph to show how the speed of the ship varied with time from the instant the towing cable was released until the ship came to rest.
iv) How far did the ship travel after the towing cable was released?

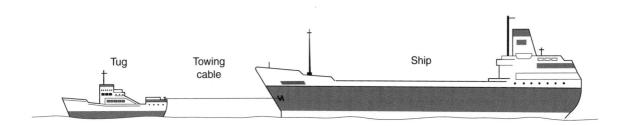

Tug     Towing cable     Ship

**3** Bales of straw were raised by an elevator from a platform, 0.5 m above the ground, onto a stack at constant speed. The stack is 5.5 m above the ground and the bales have a mass of 25 kg.

a) How much gravitational potential energy did a bale gain in being lifted from the platform to the stack?

b) The elevator can raise 20 bales of straw to the stack in 5 minutes.
i) Calculate the power output of the electric motor of the elevator during this time.
ii) Give *one* reason why the input power to the electric motor is greater than the value calculated in b) i).

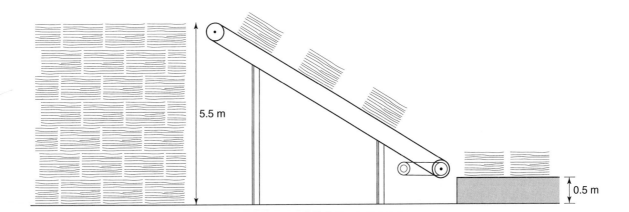

5.5 m

0.5 m

4   The driver of a train sees that the signal ahead is at red and applies the train's brakes. The diagram below shows how the speed of the train varied with time from the instant the signal was seen by the driver.

a) What was the reaction time of the driver?

b) Calculate the deceleration of the train between A and B.

c) The train was 620 m away from the signal when the driver saw it. Did the train stop in this distance? You *must* clearly show the working which leads to your answer.

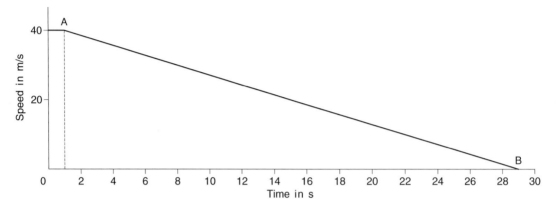

5   The diagram below shows a pendulum bob at point X, its rest position. The pendulum bob has a mass of 0.2 kg.

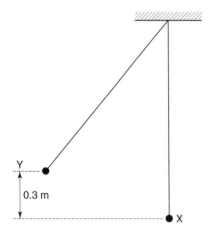

The pendulum bob was then pulled to point Y. Point Y is 0.3 m above the rest position.

a) Find the gain in gravitational potential energy of the bob when it is moved from point X to point Y.

b) The pendulum bob was released from point Y and swung to and fro until it came to rest.

i) Describe the energy changes which took place as the pendulum bob swung from point Y to point X.

ii) Show that the maximum possible speed of the pendulum bob is 2.45 m/s. State any assumption you have made in your calculation.

6   A girl of mass 45 kg starting from rest at point P skis down a ski slope. She accelerated uniformly down the slope to point Q and then moved along a level slope to point R where she stopped. Point P is 20 m vertically above point Q as shown below.

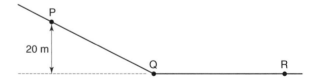

a) Calculate the change in gravitational potential energy of the girl as she moves from point P to point Q.

b) Assuming that all her gravitational potential energy was transferred to kinetic energy, calculate her speed at point Q.

c) As the girl passed point Q, her skis applied a constant retarding force of 15 N. This force caused her to decelerate to rest during the level section between points Q and R.

Calculate the distance travelled by the girl as she skied along the level section between points Q and R.

7    During a sailing competition, a boy competed in a race. The graph below shows how the speed of the boat varied with time during the race.

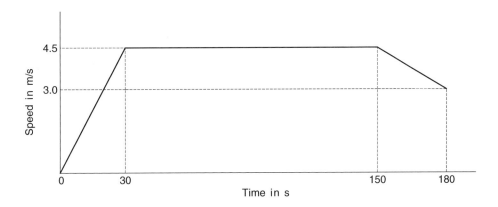

a) i) Find the acceleration of the boat during the first 30 seconds of the race.
ii) Calculate the distance travelled by the boat during the race.
iii) What was the average speed of the boat during the race?

b) The diagram below shows the horizontal forces acting on the boat during the race.

i)   During the first 30 seconds of the race are these forces balanced or unbalanced?
ii)  Between the times of 30 s and 150 s during the race are these forces balanced or unbalanced?

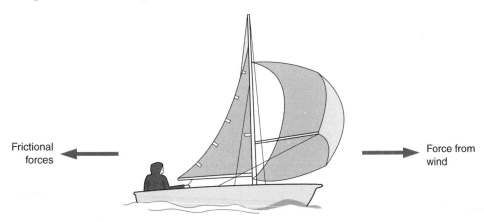

# 6 Energy Matters

*Supply and demand*

**PHYSICS** *facts*

- The fossil fuels, coal, oil and gas, are at present our main sources of energy.

- The reserves of the fossil fuels will not last for ever i.e. they are finite.

- Examples of renewable energy sources are solar, wind, hydroelectric, wave, tidal and biomass.

- Renewable energy sources have advantages and disadvantages e.g. solar energy is non-polluting but is difficult and expensive to produce in large amounts.

## QUESTIONS

**1** At present Britain's main sources are provided by the three fuels, oil, gas and coal.

a) What name is given to these sources of energy?

b) Will these sources of energy last forever?

**2** Give one example of how energy could be conserved
a) in your home
b) in transport
c) in industry.

In each case explain how less energy would be required.

**3** A small wind generator produces 80 W of electrical power.

a) How many of these generators would be required to produce 320 W of electrical power?

b) Give a reason why such small generators would not normally be suitable for supplying the power for a typical Scottish home.

**4** A number of different energy sources are listed below.

biomass, coal, gas, hydroelectric, oil, solar, wave, wind

a) List these energy sources in a table with the headings 'Renewable' and 'Non-renewable'.

b) What is meant by the terms 'renewable' and 'non-renewable'.

**5** State one advantage and one disadvantage of using the following energies
a) solar, b) wind, c) wave.

C

**6**  A large wind generator can produce 1.5 MW of electricity.

a) Suggest a suitable location for the wind generator.

b) How many of these wind generators would be required to produce 90 MW of electricity?

c) Give one disadvantage of generating electricity in this way.

**7**  The power of the waves hitting a wave generator is 60 kW per metre. The output power from the wave generator is 15 kW per metre at this time. The electrical power output of a number of the wave generators is 300 MW. What is the total length of the wave generators?

**8**  On a certain day in summer, a 1 metre square solar panel receives 200 W of solar power. The solar cells making up the panel are able to convert 20 W of the solar energy falling on them into electrical energy. Calculate the electrical energy produced by the panel in 5 hours.

## 6.2 *Generation of electricity*

- Thermal and nuclear power stations change the chemical energy of the fuel (coal, oil, gas or uranium) into electrical energy (chemical to heat to kinetic to electrical).

- A hydroelectric power station changes the gravitational potential energy of water behind a high dam into electrical energy (gravitational potential to kinetic to electrical).

- A nuclear power station produces radioactive waste.

- Nuclear fission can occur when a uranium-235 nucleus is struck by and absorbs a neutron. The uranium-235 nucleus becomes unstable and splits into two large fragments and some neutrons. The 'extra' neutrons can go on to produce further fissions.

- $\text{Efficiency} = \dfrac{\text{useful energy output}}{\text{total energy input}} \times 100\%$ or

  $\text{Efficiency} = \dfrac{\text{useful power output}}{\text{total power input}} \times 100\%$

- A chain reaction is when at least one neutron from each fission goes on to produce a further fission.

- Energy is degraded during any energy change. This means that there is less useful energy after the change than was available before the change took place.

## QUESTIONS

1   Part of a thermal power station is shown below.

Name the energy change, which takes place at a) the boiler, b) the generator.

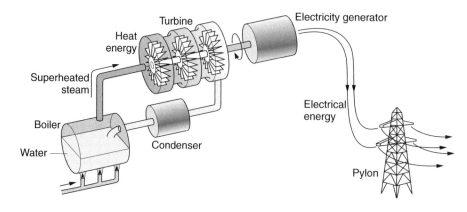

**2** The diagram below shows part of a hydroelectric power station.

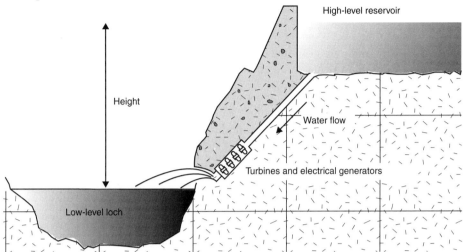

Name the energy change which takes place

a) when water goes down the pipe in the mountainside

b) at the generator.

**3** The diagram below shows part of a nuclear power station.

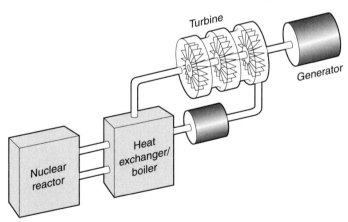

Name the energy change which takes place at a) the nuclear reactor, b) the generator.

**4** Coal-fired power stations produce a number of waste products, for example carbon dioxide, sulphur dioxide and ash. Name the main waste produced by a nuclear power station.

**5** In a small hydroelectric power station, water falls through a vertical height of 80 m. On average, 1000 kg of water passes through the turbine every 10 s.

a) How much gravitational potential energy does 1000 kg of water lose in 10 s?

b) Calculate the maximum power output from the power station.

**6** Pumped hydroelectric schemes form an important part of Scotland's power generation requirements.

a) State the main energy change which occurs when a pumped hydroelectric power station is generating electricity.

b) Describe the principle of a pumped hydroelectric power station.

7   When 1 kg of coal is burnt it produces 30 MJ of energy but 1 kg of uranium fuel produces $5 \times 10^6$ MJ of energy.

How many kilograms of coal need to be burnt to produce the same amount of energy as 1 kg of uranium fuel?

8   Copy and complete the table shown below.

| | Efficiency | Total energy input | Useful energy output |
|---|---|---|---|
| a) | | 50 J | 40 J |
| b) | | 130 kJ | 65 kJ |
| c) | 30% | 450 J | |
| d) | 20% | 0.5 J | |
| e) | 80% | | 24 MJ |
| f) | 35% | | 140 kJ |

9   Copy and complete the table shown below.

| | Efficiency | Total power input | Useful power output |
|---|---|---|---|
| a) | | 1575 MW | 630 MW |
| b) | 90% | 20 kW | |
| c) | 75% | | 30 W |
| d) | | 0.15 W | 50 mW |

10  The power input to a thermal power station is 1680 MW. The electrical power output of the power station is 800 MW.

a) How much heat energy is produced by the burning fuel each second?

b) The purpose of the power station is to produce electricity. Calculate the efficiency of the power station.

11  Water in a hydroelectric power station falls through a vertical height of 45 m. The water passes through the turbine at the rate of 1500 kg every second. The power station is able to convert 80% of the water's energy into electricity.

a) Calculate the loss in gravitational potential energy of the water every second.

b) How much electrical energy does the power station produce every second?

12  The small wind turbine on a yacht is used to charge batteries. The wind turbine is able to convert 30% of the wind's energy into electrical energy. During part of the day the wind turbine produces, at a steady rate, 6 W of electrical power.

a) Calculate the power input to the wind turbine.

b) How much electrical energy is produced in 1 hour?

13  When 1 kg of coal is burned it produces 30 MJ of heat energy. However, when 1 kg of coal is burned, it does not produce 30 MJ of electrical energy. Explain why? Use the term 'degradation' in your answer.

14  Inside the nuclear reactor of a power station, uranium-235 nuclei are bombarded by neutrons. When a uranium-235 nucleus is absorbed by a neutron, the nucleus becomes unstable and splits into two pieces.

a) What name is given to the splitting of a uranium nucleus?

b) What other particles are released as a result of the neutron being absorbed by the uranium-235 nucleus?

c) Explain what is meant by a chain reaction.

# 6.3 *Source to consumer*

- A voltage can be produced in a coil when the magnetic field near the coil changes.

- The size of the induced voltage can be increased by increasing the strength of the magnetic field, increasing the number of turns on the coil and increasing the speed of the coils through the magnetic field.

- A transformer consists of two separate coils of wire wound on an iron core.

- Transformers are used to change the size of an a.c. voltage.

- For a transformer $\dfrac{V_p}{V_s} = \dfrac{N_p}{N_s}$

- For a 100% efficient transformer $\dfrac{V_p}{V_s} = \dfrac{N_p}{N_s} = \dfrac{I_s}{I_p}$

- High voltages are used in the transmission of electrical power as this reduces the current that the transmission lines carry and so the power loss ($=I^2 R$) is reduced.

- Electrical power is distributed by the National Grid system. Electrical power produced at the power station at 25 000 V is stepped-up by a transformer to 400 000 V for efficient transmission along the transmission lines. At the other end of the transmission lines a step-down transformer reduces the voltage to 230 V for use in our homes.

## QUESTIONS

1   The diagrams given below show a loop of wire connected to a centre-zero voltmeter. The arrows indicate the direction of movement of the wire between the poles of a magnet.

a) In which diagrams will there be a reading on the voltmeter?

b) In diagram E, what changes could be made to increase the reading on the voltmeter?

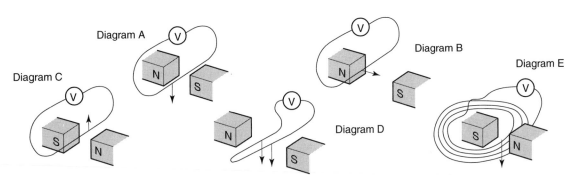

Diagram A

Diagram B

Diagram C

Diagram D

Diagram E

2 A simplified diagram of an a.c. generator is shown below.

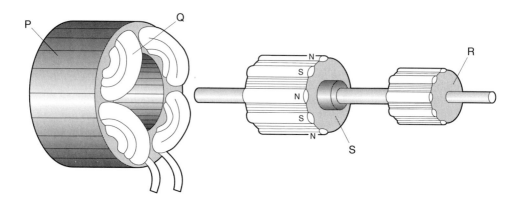

The main parts of the generator are:

dynamo (exciter), iron casing, rotor (field coils), stator.

Using the terms above, identify the parts labelled P, Q, R and S in the diagram.

3 The diagram below shows a magnet mounted on an axle, which can be rotated near a coil of wire. The coil is connected to a centre-zero voltmeter.

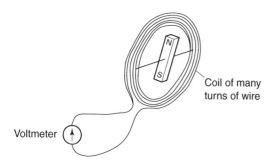

Coil of many turns of wire

Voltmeter

a) Describe what happens to the pointer on the centre-zero voltmeter when the magnet is slowly rotated near the coil.

b) When generating electricity, rotating the magnet has an important advantage to rotating the coil. What is this advantage?

c) Give three differences between a commercial generator and the simple a.c. generator shown in the diagram.

4 A student is asked to make a transformer.

a) State the purpose of a transformer.

b) Name the apparatus required and describe how the student would make the transformer.

5 Copy and complete the table shown below (assume that the transformers are all 100% efficient).

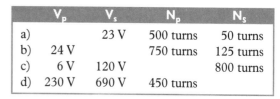

| | $V_p$ | $V_s$ | $N_p$ | $N_s$ |
|---|---|---|---|---|
| a) | | 23 V | 500 turns | 50 turns |
| b) | 24 V | | 750 turns | 125 turns |
| c) | 6 V | 120 V | | 800 turns |
| d) | 230 V | 690 V | 450 turns | |

**6** Calculate the maximum output voltage for each of the transformers shown below.

(a)
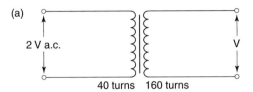
2 V a.c.      V
40 turns  160 turns

(b)
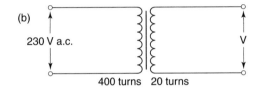
230 V a.c.     V
400 turns  20 turns

(c)
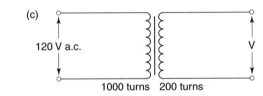
120 V a.c.     V
1000 turns  200 turns

**7** Calculate the minimum input voltage for each of the transformers shown below.

(a)

V     50 V a.c.
500 turns  200 turns

(b)
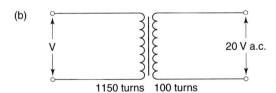
V     20 V a.c.
1150 turns  100 turns

(c)
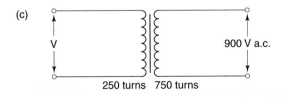
V     900 V a.c.
250 turns  750 turns

**8** Calculate the minimum number of turns that would be required on the secondary windings of the transformers shown below.

(a)
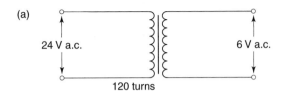
24 V a.c.     6 V a.c.
120 turns

(b)
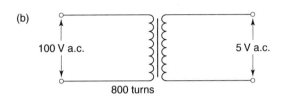
100 V a.c.     5 V a.c.
800 turns

(c)
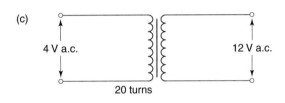
4 V a.c.     12 V a.c.
20 turns

**9** Calculate the minimum number of turns that would be required on the primary windings of the transformers shown below.

(a)
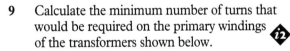
10 V a.c.     150 V a.c.
600 turns

(b)

16 V a.c.     2 V a.c.
200 turns

(c)
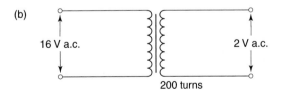
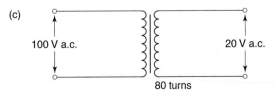
100 V a.c.     20 V a.c.
80 turns

**10** Copy and complete the table shown below (assume that the transformers are all 100% efficient).

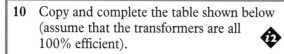

| | $V_p$ | $V_s$ | $I_p$ | $I_s$ |
|---|---|---|---|---|
| a) | | 23 V | 0.5 A | 5 A |
| b) | 120 V | | 0.01 A | 0.2 A |
| c) | 1000 V | 250 V | | 24 A |
| d) | 400 V | 10 V | 0.03 A | |

**11** Calculate the minimum current in the primary windings of the transformers shown below.

(a)

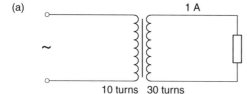

10 turns   30 turns

(b)

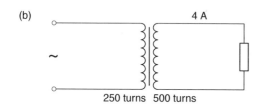

250 turns   500 turns

(c)

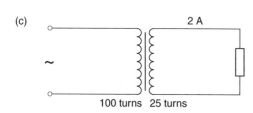

100 turns   25 turns

**12** Calculate the minimum current in the secondary windings of the transformers shown below.

(a)

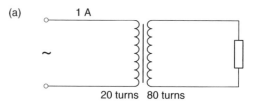

20 turns   80 turns

(b)

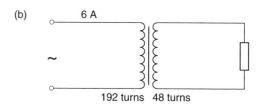

192 turns   48 turns

(c)

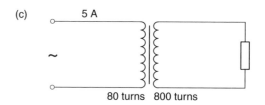

80 turns   800 turns

**13** Transformers are not 100% efficient. Give *three* reasons why some of the input energy to the transformer is wasted.

**14** High voltages, such as the 400 000 V used by the National Grid system, are extremely dangerous. Why are such high voltages used in the transmission of electricity?

**15** The National Grid system consists of a number of component parts and different voltages. The diagram below illustrates the transmission of electrical energy by the National Grid network.

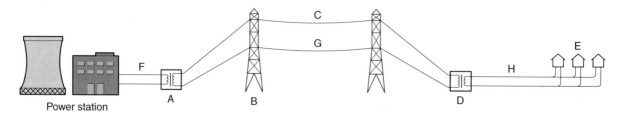

Power station

From the list (right), name the missing component parts A to E and the missing voltages F to H.

grid network, homes, pylons, step-down transformer, step-up transformer, 230 V, 25 000 V, 400 000 V

**16** A 120 V a.c. supply is connected to the 4000 turn primary coil of a transformer as shown below.

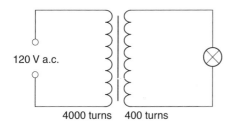

120 V a.c.

4000 turns    400 turns

A 24 W lamp is connected to the 400 turn secondary coil of the transformer. The lamp is working at its rated voltage. The transformer can be assumed to be 100% efficient.

a) Calculate the voltage the lamp is working at.

b) What current passes through the lamp?

c) Find the current in the primary coil of the transformer.

**17** The pump for a fish tank is designed to work at 10 V and 0.5 A. A transformer having a primary coil of 4600 turns is used with the 230 V supply. The transformer is 87% efficient.

a) Is the supply a.c. or d.c.?

b) How many turns are on the secondary coil of the transformer?

c) What is the output power from the transformer?

d) Calculate the input power to the transformer.

e) Calculate the current in the primary coil.

**18** A power station has an electrical power output of 500 MW. This power is transmitted along transmission cables at a voltage of 400 000 V. The transmission cables have a total length of 100 km and a resistance of 0.25 Ω per kilometre.

a) What is the current in the cables?

b) What is the resistance of 100 km of transmission cables?

c) How much power will be lost by these transmission cables?

d) How much power will be delivered to the destination?

e) What is the efficiency of the power transfer?

**19** A diagram of a model transmission system is shown below. The transformers can be considered to be ideal i.e. 100% efficient.

The transmission lines each have a resistance of 5 Ω. For the transmission lines calculate the
a) voltage across them
b) current passing through them
c) power loss from them.

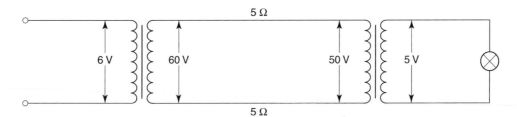

5 Ω

6 V    60 V    50 V    5 V

5 Ω

## 6.4 *Heat in the home*

- Heat always moves from a hot substance to the cooler surroundings by the processes of conduction, convection and radiation.

- Heat loss from a house depends upon the temperature difference between the inside and outside of the house and the time taken.

- Equal masses of different substances require different amounts of energy to change their temperature by 1°C.

- The energy absorbed or lost by a substance, $E_h$, is measured in joules (J), specific heat capacity, c, is measured in joules per kilogram per degree Celsius (J/kg °C), mass, m, is measured in kilograms (kg) and the change in temperature, $\Delta T$, is measured in degrees Celsius (°C).

- Energy absorbed or lost = specific heat capacity × mass
  × change in temperature

$$E_h = c\,m\,\Delta T$$

  This equation is used whenever there is a change in temperature of the substance.

- A specific heat capacity, c, of 100 J/kg °C means that 100 J of energy is required to change the temperature of 1 kg of the substance by 1°C.

- A change of state occurs when a solid changes into a liquid (or a liquid changes to a solid) or a liquid changes to a gas (or a gas changes to a liquid).

- There is no change in temperature when a change of state occurs.

- During a change in state, the energy absorbed or lost by the substance, $E_h$, is measured in joules (J), mass, m, is measured in kilograms (kg) and the specific latent heat of fusion or vaporisation, l, is measured in joules per kilogram (J/kg).

- Energy absorbed or lost = mass × specific latent heat
  $$E_h = m\,l$$

## QUESTIONS

Use the following data where necessary in the questions which follow.

| Substance | Specific heat capacity in J/kg °C |
|-----------|-----------------------------------|
| Water | 4180 |
| Copper | 386 |
| Lead | 128 |
| Aluminium | 902 |

Specific latent heat of fusion of ice = 334 000 J/kg

Specific latent heat of vaporisation of water = 2 260 000 J/kg

**1** Copy and complete the following sentences using the appropriate words from the list.

Celsius, conduction, convection, Fahrenheit, heat, radiation, temperature

A thermometer measures the _____ of an object. It uses the _____ scale in units called degrees Celsius (°C). When energy moves from one object to another, _____ from the warm object moves to the cooler object by the processes of _____ , _____ and _____ .

**2** Heat transfer can occur by the processes of conduction, convection and radiation. Which of these methods of heat transfer can take place

a) only in liquids and gases

b) through a vacuum

c) in solids, liquids and gases but not through a vacuum.

**3** Describe two ways in which heat loss can be reduced from a typical house by the processes of
a) conduction, b) convection, c) radiation.

**4** Measurements of the temperature inside and outside a house are shown in the table below.

| Day | Temp. inside in °C | Temp. outside in °C |
|---|---|---|
| Sunday | 22 | 15 |
| Monday | 20 | 10 |
| Tuesday | 19 | 8 |
| Wednesday | 21 | 12 |
| Thursday | 18 | 6 |
| Friday | 20 | 9 |
| Saturday | 21 | 14 |

On what day did the house lose most heat energy?

**5** Copper has a specific heat capacity of 386 J/kg °C. Lead has a specific heat capacity of 128 J/kg °C.

You are given equal masses of both blocks and asked to heat each one by 1°C. Which block, copper or lead, would require most heat energy? Give a reason for your answer.

**6** Calculate the amount of heat energy required to increase the temperature of
a) 2 kg of water by 2°C
b) 4 kg of water by 5°C
c) 3 kg of water by 6°C.

**7** Copy and complete the table shown below.

| | $E_h$ in J | c in J/kg°C | m in kg | ΔT in °C |
|---|---|---|---|---|
| a) | | 100 | 4 | 10 |
| b) | 5000 | | 2.5 | 5 |
| c) | 42 000 | 600 | | 14 |
| d) | 300 | 500 | 0.1 | |

**8** Calculate the amount of heat energy required to increase the temperature of 2 kg of aluminium by 50°C.

**9** A kettle is filled with 0.5 kg of water at a temperature of 20°C. Calculate the minimum amount of energy required to raise the temperature of the water to its boiling point.

**10** A 50 W electric heater takes 195 s to raise the temperature of a 1 kg aluminium block from 20°C to 30°C.

a) How much electrical energy is supplied in this time?

b) How much heat energy is absorbed by the copper block?

c) Calculate the efficiency of heating the block in this way.

**11** A small immersion heater is used to boil water in a cup. The cup holds 0.2 kg of water at an initial temperature of 20°C. The immersion heater has a power rating of 500 W. Calculate the least time it would take to boil the water.

**12** A 1 kW immersion heater is used to heat 2 kg of a liquid. The liquid had an initial temperature of 20°C. After the heater was switched on for 48 s the temperature of the liquid was 30°C. Calculate the specific heat capacity of the liquid.

**13** A tank containing 210 kg of water is heated by an immersion heater. The immersion heater is connected to the 230 V mains supply and when switched on takes a current of 30 A. The immersion heater is switched on for 24 minutes. The initial temperature of the water was 15°C.

a) Calculate the heat energy supplied by the heater.

b) Calculate the final temperature of the water.

c) In practice the water does not reach this temperature. Suggest a reason why.

**14** Give *two* examples of applications which involve a change of state.

**15** Copy and complete the following sentences using the appropriate word or terms from the list.

c m ΔT, m l, I V, fusion, specific heat capacity, vaporisation

The equation $E_h = $ _____ is used whenever a solid, liquid or gas of mass, m, undergoes a change in temperature (ΔT). The symbol c represents the _____ of the substance.

The equation $E_h = $ _____ is used whenever a change in state occurs where m is the mass of the substance which changes state. When a solid changes to a liquid at its melting point, l represents the specific latent heat of _____ . When a liquid changes to a gas at its boiling point, l represents the specific latent heat of _____ . In both cases there is no change in temperature and energy is gained (or lost) by the substance during the change of state.

**16** Copy and complete the table shown below.

| | $E_h$ | m | l |
|---|---|---|---|
| a) | | 1.5 kg | 5000 J/kg |
| b) | 50 000 J | | 200 000 J/kg |
| c) | 6680 J | 0.02 kg | |
| d) | | 100 g | 334 000 J/kg |
| e) | 45 200 J | 50 g | |

**17** How much energy is required to melt the following masses of ice at 0°C:
a) 1 kg, b) 2 kg, c) 5 kg, d) 0.8 kg?

**18** How much energy is required to vaporise the following masses of water at 100°C:
a) 1 kg, b) 2 kg, c) 5 kg, d) 0.8 kg?

**19** A 1000 W heater brings some water to its boiling point. The heater is then left on for a further 50 s. Calculate the mass of water that is boiled off in this time.

**20** A 12 V electric heater takes a current of 4 A. It is used to boil a liquid of specific latent heat of vaporisation $11.2 \times 10^5$ J/kg. The heater is left on for 8 minutes after the liquid begins to boil.

a) How much electrical energy is supplied in this time?

b) Calculate the maximum mass of liquid boiled off by the heater.

## EXAM STYLE QUESTIONS

1 A nuclear power station generates 1100 MW of electricity. The reactor of the power station uses 2 kg of uranium fuel every hour.

a) State the energy transformation which takes place when a uranium nucleus undergoes fission.

b) How much electrical energy is generated in 1 hour?

c) The energy produced when 2 kg of uranium undergoes fission is $1.08 \times 10^{13}$ J. Calculate the efficiency of the power station.

d) State one disadvantage of a nuclear power station.

2 A house has solar cells installed on its roof to provide electricity. The solar cells are installed in panels which have a total area of 5 m². On a dull day the panels receive 800 W on each square metre.

a) Calculate the total power received by the panels.

b) The panels produce 320 W of electrical power. Calculate the efficiency of the transformation.

c) i) Give one advantage of the use of solar power.
ii) Give one disadvantage of the use of solar power.

3 a) A transformer is used to step-down the 230 V mains supply to operate an a.c. motor. The primary coil of the transformer has 6250 turns and the secondary coil has 250 turns as shown below. The transformer can be assumed to be 100% efficient.

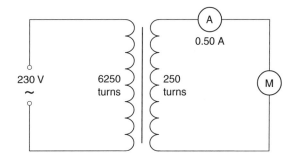

The motor lifts a 0.3 kg mass at a steady speed. The current in the secondary coil, when the mass is being lifted, is 0.50 A.
i) Calculate the current in the primary coil of the transformer when the mass is being lifted.
ii) How much electrical energy is supplied to the motor in 15 s?

b) The 0.3 kg mass is raised through a vertical height of 0.9 m in 15 s by the motor.
i) Calculate the gain in gravitational potential energy of the mass.
ii) Find the efficiency of the motor during the lifting of the mass.

4  a)  A bar magnet is suspended from a spring. The magnet can oscillate freely in and out of a coil as shown below. The coil is attached to a centre-zero voltmeter.

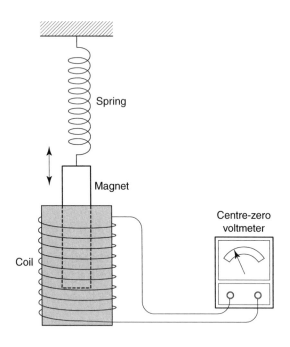

i)  The magnet is set oscillating. Describe the movement of the pointer of the centre-zero voltmeter.
ii)  Give *two* ways in which the amplitude of the movement of the pointer of the voltmeter could be made larger.

b)  Two coils of insulated wire are wound on an iron core to make a transformer as shown below.

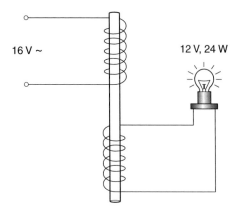

16 V ~                    12 V, 24 W

One coil is connected to a 16 V a.c. supply. The other coil is connected to a lamp, which is rated 12 V, 24 W.
i)  The lamp is operating at its correct rating. Calculate the minimum current drawn from the 16 V supply.
ii)  The current drawn from the supply is found to be 1.7 A.
A) Calculate the input power to the transformer.
B) How much electrical energy is lost by the transformer each second?
iii) Give *one* reason why a transformer is not 100% efficient.

5  A 1 kg block of a material was heated using a 50 W electric heater. The heater was switched on for 5 minutes and the temperature of the block changed from 20°C to 48°C.

a)  Calculate the specific heat capacity of the block.

b)  The specific heat capacities of some substances are shown below.

| Material | Specific heat capacity in J/kg °C |
|----------|-----------------------------------|
| Aluminium | 902 |
| Copper | 386 |
| Steel | 500 |
| Lead | 128 |

Using the table, identify the material used to make the block.

c)  The result obtained for the specific heat capacity of the material is slightly inaccurate due to energy being lost to the surroundings. What could be done to reduce the amount of heat escaping from the block by
i)  conduction?
ii)  convection?
iii) radiation?

6 An electric kettle rated at 2200 W is used to heat 1.5 kg of water. The water, at an initial temperature of 20°C, is heated to its boiling point.

a) Calculate the shortest time it will take to boil the water.

b) When the time to boil the water was measured with a stopwatch, its value was found to be longer than the value calculated in a).

Explain the differences in the times.

c) The kettle does not automatically switch off when the water boils due to a faulty thermostat. After the water has reached its boiling point, the kettle is left on for a further 100 s. Calculate the mass of water which has been changed into steam during this time.

[Specific latent heat of fusion $= 3.34 \times 10^5$ J/kg; Specific latent heat of vaporisation $= 22.6 \times 10^5$ J/kg]

# 7 Space Physics

## 7.1 *Detecting signals from space*

## QUESTIONS

1 Calculate the distance travelled in metres by light in
   a) one minute
   b) one day
   c) one year.

2 Use your answer to 1 c) to calculate the distance in metres from Earth to the nearest star which is 4.3 light years away.

**3** Use the terms below to complete the table:

galaxy, moon, planet, star, universe

| Term | Meaning |
|------|---------|
| | An object that orbits a star |
| | An object that orbits a planet |
| | A ball of gases that produces heat and light |
| | A system of stars and dust that is spinning and travelling |
| | The whole of space that can be detected |

**4** State the distance in light years from Earth to the edge of the galaxy.

**5** Copy and label the diagram to show the key features of an astronomical telescope.

**6** An object is placed 2 cm from a convex lens of focal length 3 cm as shown in the diagram.

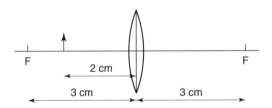

a) Copy and complete the diagram to show the final image produced by the lens.

b) Describe the image formed.

c) What is the magnification, that is the increase in size of the image compared to the object?

**7** A faint star is viewed by an optical telescope. What change should be made to the objective lens to increase the brightness of the image?

**8** White light is passed through a prism.

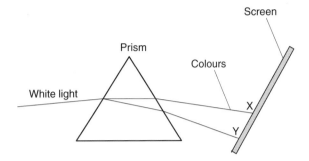

a) State the three main colours seen between X and Y.

b) Which of these colours has the longest wavelength?

**9** a) Put the following radiations in order starting with the longest wavelength:

radio, ultraviolet, infra red, visible, X-rays

b) At what speed do all these radiations travel in air?

**10** Copy and complete the table to show the detectors or radiations.

| Radiation | Detector |
|-----------|----------|
| Radio waves | |
| Infra red | |
| | The eye |
| Ultraviolet | |
| | Photographic film |
| | G-M tube |

11 A source of radiation deep in space emits waves with a frequency in the radio region of the electromagnetic spectrum.

a) What instrument can be used to detect this radio star?

b) Why is this type of instrument used rather than an optical telescope?

## INTERMEDIATE 2 QUESTIONS ONLY

12 An object of height 1 cm is placed at a distance of 30 cm from a converging lens of focal length 20 cm.

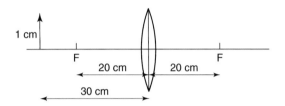

a) Copy and complete the diagram to show the final image.

b) What is the magnification of the image?

13 An object of height 5 cm is placed 50 cm from a converging lens. The lens has focal length of 20 cm.

a) By choosing a suitable scale, draw a diagram to show the rays passing through the lens and show clearly the location of the final image.

b) What is the magnification produced in this case?

14 An object is placed at 15 cm from a converging lens. The image produced by the lens is twice as large as the object and appears on the other side of the lens. By copying and completing the diagram, find the focal length of the lens.

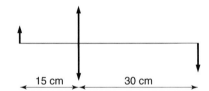

## 7.2 *Space travel*

PHYSICS *facts*

- A rocket is pushed forward because the 'propellant' is pushed back.

- A pushes B, B pushes A back.

- The force of gravity near the Earth's surface gives all objects the same acceleration (if the effects of air resistance are negligible).

- The weight of an object on the moon or on different planets is different from its weight on Earth.

- Objects in free fall appear weightless.

- The effect of friction is the transformation of $E_k$ into heat.

- Newton's Third Law is: 'If A exerts a force on B, B exerts an equal but opposite force on A'.

- Acceleration due to gravity and the gravitational field strength are the same quantities.

- Calculate the weight of an object on different planets using $W = mg$, where g is the gravitational field strength.

- The weight of a body decreases as its distance from the Earth increases.

- Projectile motion can be treated as two independent motions:
  – horizontal motion is motion at constant speed
  – vertical motion is a downward constant acceleration due to gravity.

- Satellite motion is an extension of projectile motion.

## QUESTIONS

1   A rocket is shown taking off from the Earth in the diagram below. Copy the diagram and label the two forces acting on it at take off.

2   The mass of the space shuttle is $2.0 \times 10^6$ kg and the thrust produced by the engines is $2.1 \times 10^7$ N.

a)  What is the weight of the shuttle?

b)  Show that the unbalanced force acting on the shuttle is $1 \times 10^6$ N.

c)  Calculate the acceleration of the shuttle.

3  The two objects shown below have different masses but are almost identical in volume. They are dropped from the top of a tall building.

a) What is the value of the acceleration of the objects as they fall to the ground?

b) Explain why the objects will hit the ground together.

Two objects, a feather and a hammer, are dropped on Earth. The experiment is then repeated on Mars.

c) What differences will occur in the motion of the objects?

d) Explain this difference.

4  Use the data in the table below to calculate the missing entries for different planets.

| Planet | Gravitational field strength | Mass in kg | Weight in N |
|---|---|---|---|
| Earth | 10 | 5 | |
| Moon | 1.6 | 8 | |
| Mars | | 4 | 56 |
| Saturn | | 11 | 88 |
| Jupiter | 26 | | 130 |
| Venus | 9 | | 72 |
| Mercury | 4 | | 32 |

5  A ball is tied inside a hollow can as shown and a newton balance is attached. The ball has a mass of 2.4 kg. The can has a mass of 0.1 kg.

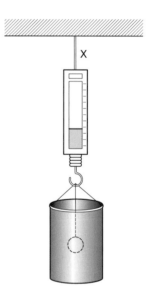

a) What will be the reading on the balance?

b) The string is cut at X.
i)  Describe the motion of the ball and the can after the string is cut.
ii) What will be the reading on the balance?

6  Newton's Third Law connects the forces between two objects. State this law.

7   The graph below shows the change in gravitational field strength with distance from the Earth.

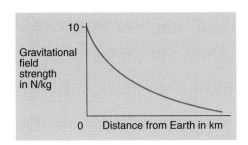

a) Explain what is meant by gravitational field strength.

b) What happens to your weight when the distance from the Earth increases?

8   A satellite is in motion around the Earth in a polar orbit. This is a low orbit with a period of 2 hours.

a) What must be done to the height of the orbit to make this a geostationary orbit?

b) Why does the satellite not fall towards the Earth?

9   In the early days of space travel the Saturn rockets and capsule would be sent into a low orbit. The early astronauts experienced a force of 8 g. Explain what is meant by 8 g.

10  When a space capsule re-entered the Earth's atmosphere, it experienced a force of air friction. What did this force do to the capsule?

11  The structure of the space shuttle is shown below.

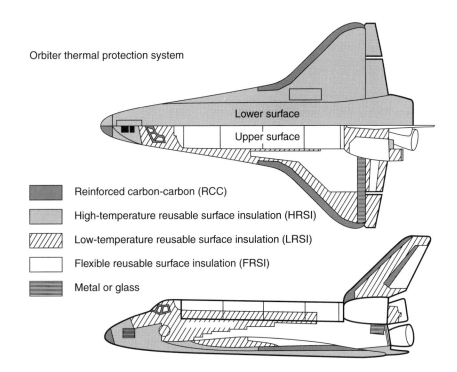

a) What is the function of the tiles on the shuttle?

b) Why are tiles on some parts of the spacecraft white while others are black?

**12** A satellite re-enters the Earth's atmosphere. It has the following information.
- Mass = 800 kg
- Initial speed = 850 m/s
- Final speed = 150 m/s
- Specific heat capacity = 1100 J/kg °C

a) Calculate the difference in kinetic energy of the satellite.

b) All this difference in kinetic energy is changed into heat energy.

How much heat energy is produced?

c) Calculate the temperature change of the satellite.

**13** A ball is projected from a cliff at 30 m/s. The time taken to land is 5 s.

a) i) Draw a speed–time graph of the horizontal speed against time.
ii) Draw a graph of vertical speed against time.

b) Calculate the horizontal distance travelled.

c) Calculate the vertical height of the cliff.

**14** A ball is thrown at 25 m/s from a roof and takes 1.75 s to land.

a) Draw a graph of horizontal speed against time.

b) Calculate the final vertical speed just before it lands.

c) What is the average vertical speed?

d) Calculate the vertical height of the building.

## EXAM STYLE QUESTIONS

**1** The Ariane 5 is a space rocket and capsule launched by the European Space Agency. The following information about the rocket and capsule is given:

- Mass of rocket and engines = 400 000 kg
- Mass of probe and heat shield = 2800 kg
- Change of temperature of heat shield on re-entry = 1100°C
- Thrust exerted by rocket engines at take off = 16 000 000 N

a) Calculate the initial acceleration of the rocket.

b) The mass of the rocket decreases as the fuel is used up.

What effect will this have on the value calculated in a)? Explain your answer.

c) The probe and heat shield enter the Earth's atmosphere with a speed of 1200 m/s. Calculate the kinetic energy of the heat shield.

d) Calculate the specific heat capacity of the shield. State any assumptions you have made in the calculations.

**2** A new star is detected which is 18 light years away.

a) What is meant by a light year?

b) One light year = $9.5 \times 10^{15}$ m. Calculate the distance travelled by the light from this star.

c) An optical telescope is used to view the star. What is the function of these parts of the telescope:
i) the objective lens
ii) the eyepiece lens?

d) To view distant stars a reflecting telescope is used which contains a large mirror. Suggest why a mirror is used rather than a lens.

**3** A star is viewed through a spectroscope and a set of coloured lines are seen on a black background.

a) What information can be obtained from these lines?

b) When another star is viewed through the same spectroscope some identical coloured lines are brighter. What does this tell you about this star compared to the first?

c) These stars are detected using a telescope which has a large diameter lens. What advantage would a large lens have over a smaller one?

**4** The original idea about satellites was thought about over 300 years ago by Sir Isaac Newton. The idea is shown in the diagram.

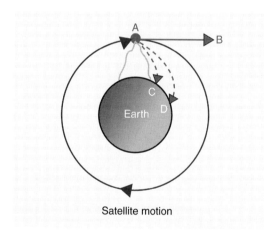

Satellite motion

a) How does this explain how a satellite can stay in orbit?

b) Over time the orbital height of the satellite decreases. What happens to the time period of the satellite?

c) As the height decreases, the speed of the satellite increases.

What will happen to the kinetic energy of the satellite?

d) Suggest what will happen to the satellite as it enters the Earth's atmosphere?

**5** On the moon an astronaut weighs 96 N.

a) Use the data sheet to find the mass of the astronaut.

b) What will she weigh on Earth?

c) Describe a situation in which she will experience weightlessness.

d) On one of the moon landings, an astronaut played golf. The path of a typical shot is shown below together with the path of a shot on Earth. Explain the difference in the paths.

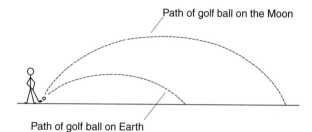

Path of golf ball on the Moon

Path of golf ball on Earth

**6** a) As you move away from the Earth, what happens to the gravitational field strength?

b) How will this affect your weight?

c) Explain why in deep space you can switch off the engines and travel at constant speed in a straight line.

# Answers

## 1 Telecommunications and Waves

### 1.1 COMMUNICATIONS USING WAVES

1  a) Light, b) Speed of light is faster than that of sound.

2  Distance of the cymbals to student B.

3  Speed = d/t = 800/2.4 = 333.3 m/s

4

| Speed in m/s | Distance in m | Time in s |
|---|---|---|
| 1500 | 1000 | **0.667** |
| 700 | 1750 | **2.5** |
| **529** | 1800 | 3.4 |
| **300** | 120 | 0.4 |
| 330 | **2310** | 7.0 |
| 560 | **1400** | 2.5 |

5  d = v × t = 340 × 3.5 = 1190 m

6

| Speed of waves in m/s | Frequency of waves in Hz | Wavelength of waves in m |
|---|---|---|
| **12** | 4 | 3 |
| **48** | 6 | 8 |
| **0.03** | 0.2 | 0.15 |
| 12 | 3 | **4** |
| 72 | 8 | **9** |
| 240 | 15 | **16** |
| 150 | **1000** | 0.15 |
| 550 | **50** | 11 |
| 340 | **20** | 17 |

7  a) i) 3 cm, ii) 10 cm = 0.1 m
   b) f = 20/50 = 0.4 Hz
   c) v = fλ = 0.4 × 0.1 = 0.04 m/s

8  a) v = fλ = 5 × 0.7 = 0.35 m/s
   b) λ = v/f = 32/8 = 4 m
   c) f = v/λ = 350/3 = 116.7 Hz

9  a) v = d/t = 160/20 = 8 m/s
   b) f = 40/20 = 2 Hz
   c) λ = v/f = 8/2 = 4 m

10  a) 3 cm, b) 1 Hz, c) v = fλ
    = 0.03 × 1 = 0.03 m/s

11  a) f = 20/(5 × 60) = 0.067 Hz,
    b) λ = v/f = 0.6/0.067 = 90 m

12  a) 512 Hz, b) λ = v/f = 340/256 = 1.33 m,
    c) t = d/v = 60/340 = 0.18 s

13  t = d/v = 170/340 = 0.5 s

14  a) Frequency decreases, b) frequency increases, c) 512 Hz

15  Frequency decreases since length increases.

16  a) i) Vibrations are at right angles to direction of energy travel, ii) vibrations are parallel to direction of energy travel
    b) Transverse is light; sound for longitudinal

### 1.2 COMMUNICATIONS USING CABLES

1  Transmitter e.g. radio source, receiver with aerial and tuner OR light source and receiver etc.

2  a) Transmitter, b) receiver

3  Telephone

4  a) i) Sound to electrical, ii) electrical to sound, b) mouthpiece and earpiece

5  a) Electrical, b) faster than the speed of sound

**6** a)

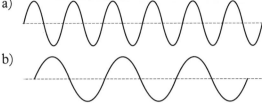

b)

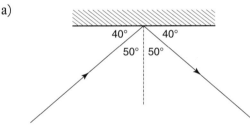

**7** a) A thin piece of solid glass drawn out as a tube.
b) In a telephone system, electrical signals from the microphone are changed into light and sent along the fibre and at the other end are changed into electrical signals to be sent to a loudspeaker.
c) The speed is faster in the cable compared with the fibre.

**8** Volume of information, speed, security (or no interference) and lower cost of fibres.

**9** a)

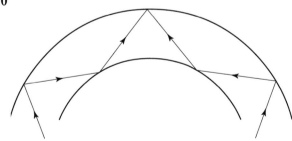

b) Reflection, c) i) 50°, ii) 50°, d) normal

**10**

**11** Microphone transmitter; modulator; laser; optical fibre; demodulator; receiver; loudspeaker

## 1.3  RADIO AND TELEVISION

**1** Aerial to receive all the signals
Decoder to remove the carrier wave
Battery to provide power to the amplifier

**2** a) Amplifier, b) energy is required to increase the amplitude of the signal

**3**

Amplitude modulated radio signal

**4** No signal is required from outside the car as the signal for the player is stored on the CD.

**5** a) Electrons scan across the screen in a series of lines. Each picture consists of 625 lines.
b) There are 25 slightly different pictures every second. The slight differences of the pictures are perceived by the eye as a moving picture.
c) The number of electrons striking the screen is the brightness. The more electrons that strike the screen the brighter the image.

**6** a) Red, blue and green
b) i) Yellow, ii) cyan

## 1.4  TRANSMISSION OF RADIO WAVES

**1** a) UHF
b) i) Medium wave,
ii) $\lambda = v/f = 300\,000\,000/810\,000$
$= 370.4$ m

**2** a) Speed of contact/availability/use in an emergency etc.
b) 300 million m/s
c) Radio wave (microwaves)

**3** a) The Earth curves so the signals cannot be sent directly.
b) To receive the incoming signal and amplify it and then re-transmit it.
c) To bring the signals to a focus and concentrate the signals into one point.

**4** a) LW = Long wave; 1500 m is the wavelength; 200 kHz is the frequency
b) $v = f\lambda = 200\,000 \times 1500$
$= 300\,000\,000$ m/s

5   a) A satellite which appears to be at the same point above the Earth all the time.
    b) Lower height

6
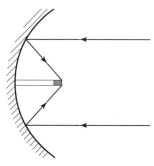

7   a) i) Station Mitchell, ii) lowest frequency means largest wavelength which has the greatest amount of bending.
    b) Diffraction

## Answers to Exam Style Questions

1   a) Lower, b) the signals will not interfere with each other.
    c) $\lambda = v/f = 300\,000\,000/6\,000\,000\,000$
    $= 0.05$ m

2   a) $\lambda = v/f = 300\,000\,000/1\,215\,000 = 247$ m
    b) Amplitude modulation, c) The combination of the high frequency carrier wave with the audio wave.

3   a) Signals cannot travel around the curve of the Earth.
    b) To receive the incoming signal and amplify it and then re-transmit it.
    c) $t = d/v = 2 \times 55\,000\,000/300\,000\,000$
    $= 0.37$ s

4   a) Electrons scan across the screen in a series of lines. Each picture consists of 625 lines.
    b) Three basic colours – red, green and blue – from three electron guns striking different coloured phosphors can combine to give all the colours.
    c) There are 25 slightly different pictures every second. The slight differences of the pictures are perceived by the eye as a moving picture.

5   a) Radio waves travel faster than other forms of communication at that time.
    b) 300 000 000 m/s
    c) $\lambda = v/f = 300\,000\,000/500\,000 = 600$ m

6   a) $d = t \times v = 4 \times 10^{-5} \times 1500 = 0.06$ m
    b) $\lambda = v/f = 1500/300\,000 = 0.005$ m. This equals 12 wavelengths so it is correct.

7   a) $t = d/v = 600/1500 = 0.4$ s
    b) i) Diffraction, ii) When frequency increases then the wavelength decreases, hence diffraction decreases.
    c) Decrease.

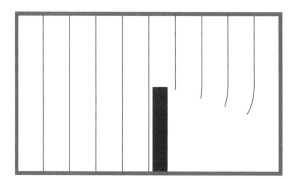

8   a) This will allow more detail on the screen since the lines will be closer.
    b) The lines run from top to bottom and as the lines build up the effect is to think that there is a complete picture.
    c) More electrons are striking the screen.

9   a) i) The speed of contact with their base.
    ii) By radio waves.
    b) More detail can be sent along with drawings.

10  a)
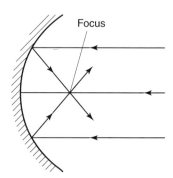

    b) The waves will come to a focus closer to the more curved dish.

# 2 *Using Electricity*

## 2.1 FROM THE WALL SOCKET

1 a) Personal stereo, b) digital clock, c) electric fire, d) food mixer, e) television.

2 a) Electrical to light, b) electrical to heat, c) electrical to kinetic, d) electrical to sound, e) electrical to heat, f) electrical to sound.

3 a) e.g. 1000 W, b) e.g. 2000 W, c) e.g. 1000 W, d) 40 W or 60 W or 100 W or 150 W.

4 a) 13 A, b) 3 A, c) 3 A, d) 13 A.

5 a) A = Neutral, B = Earth, C = Live, b) P = Blue, Q = Green/Yellow, R = Brown.

6 a) The fuse melts or 'blows'. b) Flex and/or appliance would overheat and be damaged and perhaps catch fire. c) The fuse is intended to protect the flex, however, it also protects the appliance. Should the flex (appliance) have to pass a higher current than it was designed for, then the flex (appliance) would overheat and be damaged.

7 i) P, 3 A, ii) R, 13 A, iii) S, 13 A, iv) P, 3 A, v) Q, 13 A.

8 a) Live, Neutral and Earth. b) Live and Neutral. c) A square within a square.

9 a) It is a safety device. b) Should the Live wire touch the metal casing of the appliance, then the Earth wire provides an easy path for current to pass to earth. A large current passes through the fuse, which melts or 'blows'. The electrical circuit is broken and the appliance is safe to touch.

10 a) Metal casing. b) In case the metal casing of the kettle becomes Live. The Earth wire will then provide an easy path for current to pass to earth. A large current passes through the fuse, which melts or 'blows'. The electrical circuit is broken and the appliance is safe to touch.

11 poor; increased.

12 a) Someone may be able to touch an exposed live wire. b) Someone may be able to touch an exposed live wire. c) The water, which is a conductor, may enter the appliance and then provide a path for current to pass through you to earth.

13 Socket may overheat if too large a current is drawn from it.

14 Should the fuse melt or 'blow' due to an electrical fault, then no part of the flex or appliance will remain live beyond the broken fuse.

15 The Live wire. When the switch is 'off' (open) then no part of the flex or appliance will remain live beyond the open switch.

## 2.2 ALTERNATING AND DIRECT CURRENT

1 Electrons, current, amperes, energy, volts.

2 One, one, direct, d.c., opposite, alternating, a.c.

3 50, 50, 230.

4 Less, peak, declared.

5 a) b)
  c) d)
  e) f)

6 a) b)

7 a) 30 C, b) 6 C, c) 25 A, d) 5 A, e) 40 s, f) 250 s

8 a) 75 C, b) 180 C, c) 21.6 C

9 720 C

10 40 s

11  2 A

12  5 V means 5 J of energy are given to each coulomb of charge.

13  a) The charges move in only one direction, b) The charges move in one direction, then the other direction i.e. to and fro.

14  Any value greater than 16 V e.g. 23 V

15  230 V

16  50 Hz

17  a) Switch, b) fuse, c) resistor, d) battery, e) variable resistor, f) lamp.

18  a) Capacitor, b) diode.

## 2.3  RESISTANCE

1

(a)   (b)

2  a) Voltmeter, b) ammeter.

3  a) and b) Ammeter connected in series anywhere in circuit; voltmeter connected in parallel with R.

4  Resistance, ohms, decreases, electrical, heat.

5  Constant

6  e.g. television, radio, hi-fi.

7  a) 10 V, b) 12 V, c) 0.05 A, d) 5.75 A, e) 2 $\Omega$, f) 400 $\Omega$

8  a) 12 V, b) 0.5 A, c) 2 $\Omega$

9  12 V

10  6 $\Omega$

11  0.25 A

12  17.7 $\Omega$

13  4 $\Omega$

14  e.g. cooker, toaster, kettle, electric fire.

15  joules, watts, divided, joules, second.

16  a) 24 W, b) 115 W, c) 2 A, d) 9.57 W, e) 9 V, f) 230 V

17  a) 48 W, b) 48 J

18  a) 2300 W, b) 1265 W, 920 W

19  a) Filament – electrical to heat and light in the filament wire; discharge – electrical to light in the gas, b) discharge lamp, c) 100 J

20  a) i) Electrical to heat, ii) element of heater, b) 4.6 A, c) 1058 W

21  $V = I \times R. P = I \times V = I \times (I \times R) = I^2 \times R$

22  a) 60 W, b) 0.9 W, c) 46 $\Omega$, d) 30 $\Omega$, e) 3 A, f) $5 \times 10^{-3}$ A

23  5 W

24  23 $\Omega$

25  4 A

## 2.4  USEFUL CIRCUITS

1  a) Series, b) parallel, c) series, d) parallel.

2  a) Same, b) supply voltage = sum of voltages round circuit = $V_1 + V_2 + \ldots$

3  a) Current from supply = sum of currents in the branches = $I_1 + I_2 + \ldots$, b) same.

4  a) All 4 A, b) 2 A, 6 A, 1 A, 6 A

5  a) 110 V, b) 12 V, c) 5 V, d) 4 V

6  a) 1.5 A, 7 V, b) 5 A, 10 V, c) 2 A, 6 V

7  a) 35 $\Omega$, b) 28 $\Omega$, c) 180 $\Omega$

8  a) 6 $\Omega$, b) 12 $\Omega$, c) 15 $\Omega$

9  a) 30 $\Omega$, b) 74 $\Omega$, c) 8 $\Omega$

10  Socket will overheat if too large a current is drawn from it.

11  a) e.g. kettle, television, b) washing machine (mains + on/off + programme switch)

12  a)

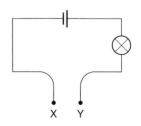

b) When X and Y are touched together, the lamp should light, c) Fuse is connected between X and Y. If fuse is blown then the lamp will not light, otherwise the lamp will light.

**13**

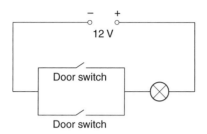

**14**

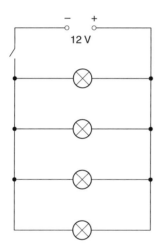

**15**

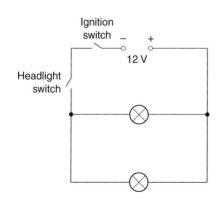

**16** a) i) Zero, ii) short, b) i) Usually the number '1' on the left hand side of display. This means value is too big to display i.e. infinite resistance, ii) open

## 2.5 BEHIND THE WALL

1 In parallel. The appliances will have the same voltage across them and if one appliance was switched off this would not affect any other appliances. Neither would be true for appliances connected in series.

2 Mains fuses protect the mains wiring from overheating.

3 a) An automatic switch which can be used instead of a fuse, b) To protect the mains wiring from overheating.

4 a) See Question 8, diagram B, b) A lighting circuit has thinner cables; is able to handle less power; has a smaller fuse than a ring circuit.

5 1 kWh = 1000 Wh = 1000 × (60 × 60) Ws = 3 600 000 Ws = 3 600 000 J since 1 W = 1 J/s

6 a) Circuit breaker, b) Fuses can be replaced with the wrong value, circuit breakers cannot.

7 a) 3 kWh, b) 24 p

8 a) 9 A, b) 4.5 A, c) Diagram B, d) Current is smaller; less heat is produced; circuit is safer; wiring can be thinner; less costly.

## 2.6 MOVEMENT FROM ELECTRICITY

1 a) C, b) B, c) D, d) A

2 a) There is a magnetic field surrounding the current-carrying wire.
b) i) Compass needles return to their original positions as shown in Diagram A, ii) Compass needles point in the opposite direction i.e. anti-clockwise.

3 Increase voltage (current); wind more turns of wire round the nail.

4 Increase voltage (current); increase number of turns of wire; place iron core through the coil.

5 Electric bell; magnetic relay.

**6** a) There is a force on the rod, towards the magnet. This is due to the interaction of the magnetic fields, due to the current-carrying wire and the permanent magnet. b) Reverse the connections to the battery; turn magnet so that magnetic field is reversed.

**7** a) i) Clockwise, ii) Reverse the connections to the battery; turn magnet so that magnetic field is reversed, b) To make good electrical contact between the battery and the commutator, c) It is an automatic switch. It reverses the direction of the current through the coil every half revolution.

**8** a) Gives good electrical contact; reduces wear on commutator, b) Gives a greater turning effect; gives smoother running; c) Gives a stronger magnet than a permanent magnet of the same size.

# Answers to Exam Style Questions

**1** a) N = Blue, E = Green/Yellow, L = Brown, b) 6 A, c) i) Live and Neutral, ii) Large current will pass through the Earth wire to earth. This causes the fuse wire to melt or 'blow'. The electrical supply is now cut off and the iron is safe to touch.

**2** a) i) 9 V, ii) 2 $\Omega$, b) i) 3 $\Omega$, ii) 4 A

**3** a) Smaller current; less heating; safer; thinner cables; less costly; b) i) 230 V, ii) 29 A, c) Cannot be replaced by a wrong/higher value of fuse.

**4** a) i) Battery, ii) Increase voltage (current); more turns of wire on coil; stronger magnet; iii) It is an automatic switch, to change the direction of the current through the coil every half revolution and allow continuous rotation of the coil. b) i) A = Commutator; B = Field coils; C = Rotating coils; D = Brushes; ii) B

**5** a) If one lamp breaks then the others remain lit; b) i) 24 $\Omega$, ii) 6 $\Omega$, c) i) 4 A, ii) 5 A

# 3 Health Physics and Radiations

## 3.1 THE USE OF THERMOMETERS

**1** The liquid expands as temperature increases.

**2** Smaller range of temperatures and has a kink in the tube.

**3** The thermometer is shaken and can then be placed in the mouth. After a short time it is removed and the reading is noted.

**4** a) 37°C, b) The temperature is below normal temperature and there is a danger of frostbite and of unconsciousness.
c) Hypothermia

## 3.2 USING SOUND

**1** The bell amplifies the frequencies from the lungs.

**2** a) Frequencies beyond the range of normal hearing i.e. greater than 20 000 Hz.
b) Examination of a foetus; shattering kidney stones etc.

**3** $\lambda = v/f = 1500/5\,000\,000 = 0.0003$ m

**4**

| Substance | Speed of sound in m/s | Frequency in Hz | Wavelength in m |
|-----------|----------------------|-----------------|-----------------|
| Air | 340 | 30 000 | 0.00113 |
| Bone | 4000 | $1 \times 10^6$ | 0.004 |
| Tissue | 1500 | 750 000 | $2 \times 10^{-3}$ |
| Fat | 1450 | 290 000 | $5 \times 10^{-3}$ |
| Blood | 1600 | $5 \times 10^5$ | $3.2 \times 10^{-3}$ |

**5** $t = d/v = 0.005/1570 = 3.2 \times 10^{-6}$ s

**6** $f = v/\lambda = 1450/0.0005 = 2.9 \times 10^6$ Hz

**7** a) 60 dB, b) 90 dB

**8** TV, Hi-fi etc.

**9** The protectors reduce the noise level.

## 3.3   LIGHT AND SIGHT

**1**

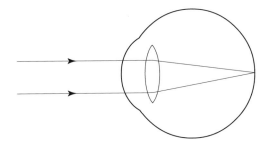

**2**    a) Refraction is when light travels from one substance to another.
b)

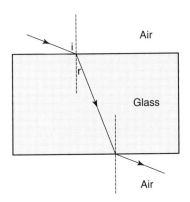

**3**    Upside down, since light travels in straight lines through the lens of the eye.

**4**    a) A convex lens; a window frame; a card
b) The lens is moved until the window frame is in focus on the card.
c) Measure the distance from the lens to the card.

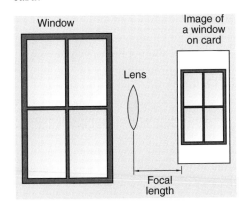

**5**

| Type of lens | Focal length in cm | Power of lens in D |
|---|---|---|
| Convex | 10 | 10 |
| Convex | 15 | 6.67 |
| Convex | 25 | 4 |
| Concave | 10 | −10 |
| Concave | 20 | −5 |

**6**    a) 0.067 m, convex   b) 0.05 m, convex
c) 0.2 m, concave

**7**    a) Short sight, b) Concave
c)

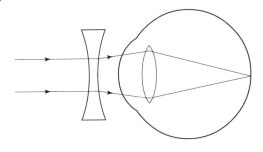

d) Long sight. e) The lens bends the light more so that the rays are brought to a focus at the retina.

**8**    a) A thin piece of glass.
b) No heat inside the body.

## 3.4 & 3.5   USING THE SPECTRUM AND RADIATION

**1**    Removing tattoos; use as a scalpel; correcting various eye defects etc.

**2**    a) To show up breaks in the bones etc. b) On film

**3**    The image is in three dimensions/more detail.

**4**    a) Ultraviolet. b) It may cause skin cancer

**5**    Infra red

**6**    It destroys the malignant cells.

**7**    To check the operation of the kidneys; bone scan etc.

**8**

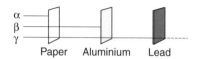

α
β
γ

Paper    Aluminium    Lead

**9**

| Statement | Particle | Charge |
|---|---|---|
| a) Found outside the nucleus | Electron | Negative |
| b) Found inside the nucleus; opposite charge to a) | Proton | Positive |
| c) Other particle in the nucleus | Neutron | No charge |

**10** a) Addition or removal of an electron to produce a charged particle.
b) Alpha radiation

**11** A film blackens with radiation and the degree of blackening increases with the amount of radiation.

**12** a) Becquerel, b) The activity decreases.

**13** a) The time taken for the activity to fall to half of its initial value. b) Halving the 10 MBq successively gives 5, 2.5, 1.25, 0.625, i.e. four half-lives. This equals 24 hours. One half-life is 6 hours.

**14** 15.2/3.8 = four half-lives. 50 kBq halved four times is 3.13 kBq.

**15** 17 190 years/5730 = three half-lives
Halving 70 mg three times gives 35, 17.5, 8.75.
Amount left is 8.75 mg.

**16** 15.9/5.3 = three half-lives. 50 mg halved three times is 25, 12.5, 6.25. Activity is 6.25 kBq.

**17** Halving 100 continuously gives 50, 25, 12.5, 6.25 i.e. four times giving four half-lives. Four half-lives = 10.8 days.
One half-life = 10.8/4 = 2.7 days

**18** Do not eat in the lab; do not point the source at anyone; no-one under 16 allowed to handle sources.

**19** a) Sievert, b) Type and the energy of the radiation.

**20** a) Becquerel, b) gray, c) sievert

**21** $E = m \times D = 70 \times 10 = 700$ J

**22** a) A measure of the biological effect on tissue.
b) $25 \times 10^{-6} \times 1 = 25 \times 10^{-6}$ Sv

**23** For alpha, $H = DQ =$
$20 \times 10 \times 10^{-6} = 200$ µSv
For gamma, $H = 25 \times 10^{-6} \times 1 = 25$ µSv
Total, $H = 225$ µSv

**24** Cosmic rays, granite rocks, radon gas etc.

# Answers to Exam Style Questions

**1** a) Excimer, b) $E = Pt = 15 \times 5 = 75$ J
c) Removing tattoos; use as a scalpel etc.

**2** a) i) Short sight, ii) concave
b) Focal length = 1/power = 1/3.25 = 0.31 m

**3** a) Frequencies beyond the range of hearing
b) $\lambda = v/f = 1600/4\,000\,000 = 0.0004$ m
c) $75 \times 0.0004 = 0.03$ m

**4** a) 90 dB b) 60 dB

**5** a) Infra red, b) Longer, c) i) For the production of vitamin D
ii) It may cause skin cancer

**6** a) Alpha and gamma
b) i) Gain or loss of an electron to produce a charged particle
ii) It will produce a large ionisation density which is dangerous.

**7** a) i) Gamma radiation is penetrating radiation which is only reduced by lead or concrete.
ii) This is the time taken for the activity of the source to reach half of its initial activity.
b) Gamma radiation is the only radiation which can penetrate through the skin and tissue. Other radiations are absorbed.
c) The tumour is always receiving radiation but the other tissue is only receiving a fraction of the radiation.

**8** a) Black since the radiation will pass through the break in the bone
b) i) To see the image in three dimensions.
ii) $20 \times 8 = 160$ mm
c) Heat

# 4 *Electronics*

## 4.1 OVERVIEW

**1** Input, process and output.

**2** a) Digital, b) analogue, c) analogue, d) digital.

**3** A digital signal has only one of two possible values; an analogue signal can have any possible value.

## 4.2 OUTPUT DEVICES

**1** e.g. LED – electrical to light; relay – electrical to the opening or closing of a switch.

**2** e.g. loudspeaker – electrical to sound; motor – electrical to kinetic.

**3**

**4** P, LED does not light; Q, LED lights; R, LED does not light (LED damaged).

**5** a) P = LED, Q = resistor; b) To prevent too large a current (or voltage) from damaging the LED.

**6** 1, 3, 4, 5, 7 and 9

**7** a) Solenoid, b) motor, c) buzzer or lamp or LED, d) buzzer or lamp or LED

**8** a) See circuit in Question 5 but with a 9 V battery, b) 600 Ω

**9** a) 2, b) 8, c) 7, d) 9

## 4.3 INPUT DEVICES

**1** a) Sound to electrical, b) heat to electrical, c) light to electrical

**2** a) Capacitor, b) solar cell, c) LDR or solar cell, d) thermocouple or thermistor, e) microphone

**3** a) 10 000 Ω, b) The value changes. It depends on the type of thermistor but would usually be less than 10 000 Ω.

**4** Less than 2000 Ω

**5** a) 2000 Ω, 1111 Ω, 714 Ω, b) Resistance goes down with increasing light intensity, c)

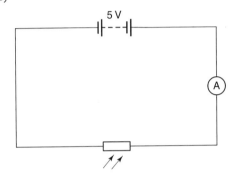

**6** a) 50 Ω, b) 6 V and a value less than 0.12 A e.g. 0.10 A

**7** a) It increases with time to 12 V, b) i) 1 μF + 10 kΩ, ii) 10 μF + 100 kΩ

**8** a) Thermistor or thermocouple, b) capacitor, c) microphone, d) LDR or solar cell

**9** a) 30 Ω, b) 0.3 A, c) i) 3 V, ii) 6 V

**10** a) 2.5 V, 2.5 V; b) 2 V, 4 V, c) 3.33 V, 16.67 V

**11** a) 12 V, 24 Ω, b) 3 V, 60 Ω, c) 4 V, 4000 Ω

**12** a) 10 Ω, 6 V, b) 24 Ω, 100 V, c) 250 Ω, 7 V

## 4.4  DIGITAL PROCESSES

**1**  a) W = thermistor, X = resistor, Y = transistor, Z = lamp, b) An electronic switch

**2**  a) On (conducting), b) The LED goes out. The transistor is off (non-conducting).

**3**  a) i) Zero, ii) Off (non-conducting), iii) Unlit, b) The capacitor begins to charge and the voltmeter reading rises. When the voltmeter reading $\geqslant 0.7$ V, the LED lights.

**4**  i) a) e.g. to switch on the lamp when it gets dark, b) e.g. the LED lights when a cooker element is hot, c) the LED lights after a time delay e.g. electronic egg timer

ii) The variable resistor allows each circuit to be adjusted to different conditions.

**5**  a)  As the temperature increases, the resistance of the thermistor decreases, so there will be less voltage across the thermistor. This means that the voltage across resistor R increases and when it $\geqslant 0.7$ V, the transistor switches on and the buzzer sounds.
b)  Same diagram as given in the question but with the positions of the thermistor and resistor R interchanged.

**6**  In moving to the dimly lit room, the resistance of the LDR increases. The voltage across the LDR increases and when it $\geqslant 0.7$ V, the transistor switches on and the LED lights.

**7**  See Section 4 Physics Facts

**8**  See Section 4 Physics Facts

**9**  See Section 4 Physics Facts

**10**  See Section 4 Physics Facts

**11**  A truth table shows the output for all the possible input combinations.

**12**  Logic '1' = high voltage (HIGH); logic '0' = low voltage (LOW)

**13**  A = OR gate, B = NOT gate, C = AND gate

**14**

| C | D |
|---|---|
| 0 | 1 |
| 1 | 0 |
| 1 | 0 |
| 1 | 0 |

**15**

| D | E | F |
|---|---|---|
| 0 | 0 | 0 |
| 0 | 1 | 0 |
| 1 | 0 | 0 |
| 1 | 1 | 1 |
| 1 | 0 | 0 |
| 1 | 1 | 1 |
| 1 | 0 | 0 |
| 1 | 1 | 1 |

**16**

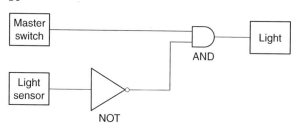

**17**

**18**  a) i) Zero, ii) X is logic '0' and Y is logic '1', iii) 6 V, b) i) Voltage increases with time, ii) X will change to logic '1' and Y to logic '0', c) i) Voltage decreases with time, ii) X will change back to logic '0' and Y to logic '1', iii) Cycle will begin again and continue repeating.

**19** a) A series of digital pulses, b) clock pulses, c) When X is at logic '0', then Y is at logic '1'. This means that the capacitor will charge up and the voltage across it increases with time until the logic at X changes to logic '1' and so Y becomes logic '0'. The capacitor will now discharge and the voltage across it decreases with time until the logic at X changes to logic '0' and so Y becomes logic '1'. The cycle now repeats, d) decrease value of resistor or decrease value of capacitor.

**20** a) Binary counter, b) e.g. an electronic clock/watch

**21** a) Binary, b) decimal

## 4.5   ANALOGUE PROCESSES

**1** Baby alarm, hi-fi, radio, television.

**2** a) To make the electrical signal larger, b) same, c) output signal > input signal

**3** a) 500, b) 600, c) 15 V, d) 45 V, e) 0.04 V, f) $2.5 \times 10^{-5}$ V

**4** 150

**5** 15 V

**6** $6 \times 10^{-5}$ V

**7** Connect a voltmeter across the input to the amplifier and another voltmeter across the output from the amplifier. Note readings from voltmeters. Calculate voltage gain of amplifier using the equation

$$\text{voltage gain} = \frac{\text{output voltage}}{\text{input voltage}}$$

**8** a) 50, b) 600, c) 0.8 W, d) $6.75 \times 10^{-3}$ W, e) 0.006 W, f) $6 \times 10^{-6}$ W

**9** 1500

**10** 25 W

**11** $2.5 \times 10^{-6}$ W

**12** a) 0.25 W, b) 7.2 W, c) 0.08 Ω, d) 52.9 Ω, e) 3 V, f) 10 V

**13** $1.2 \times 10^{-10}$ W

**14** a) 9.6 W, b) 12 V

**15** a) 25 kΩ, b) $9.4 \times 10^{8}$

# Answers to Exam Style Questions

**1**  a) i)

| Input devices | Output devices |
|---|---|
| microphone | loudspeaker |
| switch | LED |
| LDR | motor |
| thermistor | |
| capacitor | |

ii) sound to electrical
b) i) W = thermistor, X = resistor, Y = transistor, Z = lamp, ii) to switch on a lamp when it gets warm e.g. light comes on when temperature in a freezer gets too high.

**2** a) i) 8 V, ii) 1500 Ω, b) 200 units, c) As the light intensity decreases, the resistance of the LDR increases. The voltage across the LDR increases and when it is equal to or greater than 0.7 V then the transistor switches on and the lamp lights.

**3** a) Y, b) 900 Ω

**4** a) i) OR gate, ii) AND gate
b)

| D | E |
|---|---|
| 0 | 0 |
| 1 | 1 |
| 1 | 1 |
| 1 | 1 |

**5** a) a.c. voltage, b) 35, c) 500 Hz

# 5 *Transport*

## 5.1 ON THE MOVE

1 Note initial distance (odometer) reading before journey. Note final distance (odometer) reading after journey. Start stopwatch when journey starts and stop it when journey is completed. Note time taken for journey. Calculate distance travelled from final distance reading – initial distance reading.

$$\text{Calculate average speed} = \frac{\text{distance travelled}}{\text{time taken}}$$

2 a) 10 m/s, b) 5 m/s, c) 20 s, d) 50 s, e) 90 m, f) 12 000 m

3 4 m/s

4 1500 m

5 12.5 s

6 25 m/s

7 3750 s

8 6 cm

9 e.g. mark a line on the road. Start a stopwatch when the front of the bicycle passes this line and stop stopwatch when rear of bicycle passes the line. Measure length of bicycle.

$$\text{Calculate speed} = \frac{\text{length of bicycle}}{\text{time on stopwatch}}$$

10 Average speed is the total distance travelled divided by the total time taken for the journey. Instantaneous speed is the speed of an object, at a certain time during the journey.

11 a) Speed = the distance travelled in 1 s
b) Acceleration = the change in speed in 1 s

12 a) 3 m is travelled in 1 s, b) 10 cm is travelled in 1 s, c) 150 km is travelled in 1 hour

13 a) The speed of the object increases by 2 m/s every second, b) the speed of the object increases by 10 m/s every second, c) the speed of the object decreases by 4 m/s every second.

14 a) 4 m/s$^2$, b) 0.5 m/s$^2$, c) 16 m/s, d) 10 m/s, e) 4 s, f) 15 s

15 4 miles per hour per second

16 a) 2 m/s$^2$, b) 1 m/s$^2$, c) 4 m/s$^2$, d) $-1$ m/s$^2$, e) 16 m/s, f) 3 s, g) 27 m/s, h) 2 s

17 a) 4.5 m/s, b) 7.5 m/s, c) 15 m/s

18 1.8 m/s$^2$

19 0.167 m/s$^2$

20 a) 10 m/s, b) 0.4 m/s$^2$

21 4 s

22 5 miles per hour per second

23

24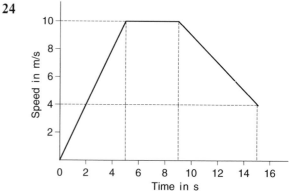

25 a) Constant speed, b) constant acceleration, c) constant deceleration, d) constant acceleration

26 a) 1.25 m/s$^2$, b) $-1.4$ m/s$^2$, c) 0.4 m/s$^2$, d) $-1.5$ m/s$^2$

27 a) 60 m, 2.5 m/s$^2$, 0, b) 54 m, 0, $-3$ m/s$^2$, c) 96 m, 4 m/s$^2$, 0, $-2.4$ m/s$^2$, d) 77.5 m, 1 m/s$^2$, 0, $-3$ m/s$^2$

28  a) i) Constant acceleration, ii) constant deceleration, b) i) 10 m/s$^2$, ii) $-10$ m/s$^2$, c) 3.6 m, d) 1.8 m

29  a) i) Constant acceleration, ii) constant speed, iii) constant deceleration, b) i) 2 m/s$^2$, ii) 0, iii) $-1.25$ m/s$^2$, c) 560 m, d) 13.7 m/s

30  a) In Method A, the student has to judge when the front of the trolley reaches point X and so start the stopwatch and judge when the rear of the trolley reaches point X to stop the stopwatch.
In Method B, the timer starts when the trolley breaks the beam at point X and stops when the trolley passes through the light beam.
b) Method B

## 5.2    FORCES AT WORK

1   Change the speed, direction and/or the shape of an object.

2   Attach newton balance to the object. Pull on newton balance until object is at rest. The reading on the newton balance is now equal to the force applied to the object.

3   Weight, newtons, Earth, gravitational

4   a) 20 N, b) 54 N, c) 3.5 kg, d) 0.5 kg, e) 10 N/kg, f) 10 N/kg

5   50 N

6   0.6 kg

7   a) 600 N, b) 60 kg, c) 96 N

8   1140 N

9   Mass is the quantity of matter and is measured in kg. Weight is the pull of the Earth on an object. It is a force and is measured in N.

10  a) North, b) South

11  a) e.g. to stop a car and a bicycle by using the brakes, b) e.g. to allow a car to accelerate by releasing the brakes, lubricating a surface.

12  Opposite, no, balanced, constant

13  'An object will remain at rest or move at constant speed in a straight line unless acted on by an unbalanced force'

14  Engine force in the same direction as the car is travelling. Force of friction in opposite direction.

15  a) 12 N, b) 12 N upwards. From Newton's First Law, since the lamp shade is stationary, then there must be balanced forces acting on it. One force is the weight acting downwards. Hence, the tension must be equal in size but in the opposite direction to the weight.

16  a) Weight of parachutist is equal in size but in the opposite direction to the frictional force of the air.
b) Weight of clock is equal in size but in the opposite direction to the force (reaction) of the table.
c) Pedalling force is equal in size but in the opposite direction to the frictional force.

17  When the brakes are applied, then a force acts in the opposite direction of motion on the car or bus, which decelerates. This force does not act on the person and so they would continue to travel at constant speed in a straight line. However, the seat belt applies a force, in the same direction as the braking force, which decelerates the person.

18  a) 4 N, b) 4 N, c) 0 N, d) 30 N

19  a) 15 N, b) 1.4 N, c) 0.33 m/s$^2$, d) 25 m/s$^2$, e) 30 kg, f) 6 kg

20  3000 N

21  1.5 m/s$^2$

22  80 000 kg

23  a) 2 m/s$^2$, b) 1.5 kg, c) 1.5 N, d) 11 N

24  a) 1.5 N, b) 0.5 N

25  a) 3240 N, b) 3740 N

26  a) As mass decreases, the acceleration increases, b) As the unbalanced force decreases, the acceleration decreases.

## 5.3 MOVEMENT MEANS ENERGY

1 a) Chemical to kinetic, b) chemical to heat, c) kinetic to heat

2 a) Chemical to gravitational potential, b) gravitational potential to kinetic

3 Work, gravity, gravitational, kinetic, greater

4 a) 10 J, b) 25 m, c) 50 N, d) 150 J, e) 0.33 m, f) 250 N

5 150 J

6 75 N

7 30 m

8 250 m

9 240 N

10 a) 3000 N, b) $1.5 \times 10^6$ J

11 a) 100 W, b) 3000 J, c) 40 s, d) 0.2 W, e) 12 000 J, f) 200 s

12 140 W

13 1440 J

14 5 s

15 a) 4 J, b) 5 kg, c) 5 m/s, d) 320 J, e) 80 kg, f) 0.3 m/s

16 45 J

17 2.16 kg

18 2 m/s

19 0.001 J

20 0.2 kg

21 30 m/s

22 a) 60 J, b) 0.9 m, c) 2.5 kg, d) 4 J, e) 6 m, f) 2 kg

23 75 J

24 1.8 m

25 2.5 kg

26 600 J

27 a) 75 J, b) 75 J, c) 10 m/s

28 a) 1440 J, b) 1440 J, c) 3.2 m

29 a) 50 000 J, b) 1666.7 W

30 a) $1.75 \times 10^6$ J, b) 35 000 W

## 5.4 MECHANICS AND HEAT – KINEMATICS

1 Distance has magnitude (size) only. Displacement has magnitude (size) and direction.

2 Speed has magnitude (size) only. Velocity has magnitude (size) and direction.

3 a) A scalar quantity has magnitude (size) only, a vector quantity has magnitude (size) and direction.
b) Scalar: distance, speed; Vector: displacement, velocity

4

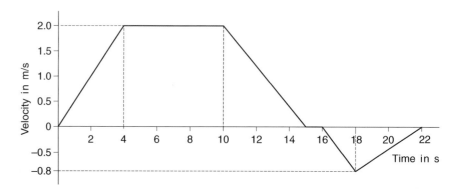

**5** a) i) Constant acceleration; ii) constant acceleration; b) 1.25 m; c) 0.45 m; d) 0.5 s; the time when the velocity changes from positive to negative i.e. when ball changes direction as a result of hitting the ground.

**6** Total momentum before = Total momentum after, 35 v = 20 × 3.8, v = 2.2 m/s

**7** Total momentum before = Total momentum after, 62 × 3.5 = 115 v, v = 1.9 m/s

**8** Total momentum before = Total momentum after, 1200 × 15 = 2000 v, v = 9 m/s

## Answers to Exam Style Questions

**1** a) Susan puts a line on the road. She places another line, for example, 10 m from the first line. When Lynne reaches the first line, Susan starts the stopwatch and when Lynne reaches the second line she stops the stopwatch. She calculates the average speed using

$$\text{Average speed} = \frac{\text{distance between the two lines}}{\text{time on stopwatch}}$$

b) i) 150 N, ii) 120 J

**2** a) 1200 N, b) i) 0.005 m/s$^2$, ii) 300 s, iii)

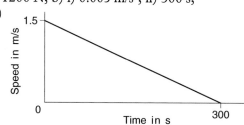

iv) 225 m

**3** a) 1250 J, b) i) 83.3 W, ii) Energy is lost as heat and sound

**4** a) 1 s, b) 1.43 m/s$^2$, c) Yes, train stopped in 600 m

**5** a) 0.6 J, b) i) Gravitational potential energy is changed into kinetic energy, heat and sound, ii) Assume no energy is changed into heat and sound.

**6** a) 9000 J, b) 20 m/s, c) 600 m

**7** a) i) 0.15 m/s$^2$, ii) 720 m, iii) 4 m/s, b) i) unbalanced; ii) balanced

# 6 Energy Matters

## 6.1 SUPPLY AND DEMAND

**1** a) Fossil fuels, b) No

**2** a) e.g. fit draught excluders – less heat energy lost from home so smaller fuel consumption, b) e.g. cycle or walk to school – less fuel used by vehicles required to take you to school, c) e.g. recycle waste products – less energy required in the production of new materials.

**3** a) 4, b) Power output from these generators is too small for a typical home and/or wind energy is very variable.

**4** a)

| Renewable | Biomass | Hydroelectric | Solar | Wave | Wind |
|---|---|---|---|---|---|
| Non-renewable | Coal | Gas | Oil | | |

b) Renewable means that they cannot be used up; non-renewable means that they will eventually be used up.

**5** a), b) and c) Last for ever/clean, variable.

**6** a) Top of a hill or a windy location, b) 60, c) If no wind, then no electricity is generated/unsightly.

**7** 20 000 m

**8** 360 000 J

## 6.2 GENERATION OF ELECTRICITY

**1** a) Chemical to heat, b) kinetic to electrical.

**2** a) Gravitational potential to kinetic, b) kinetic to electrical.

**3** a) Chemical to heat, b) kinetic to electrical.

**4** Radioactive waste

5   a) 800 000 J, b) 80 000 W

6   a) Gravitational potential to electrical,
    b) During the peak times of the day, it
    produces electricity. During the night, when
    there is excess electricity available, it uses
    electrical energy from the National Grid to
    pump water back up the mountainside ready
    for use the next day.

7   $1.67 \times 10^5$ kg

8   a) 80%, b) 50%, c) 135 J, d) 0.1 J, e) 30 MJ,
    f) 400 kJ

9   a) 40%, b) 18 kW, c) 40 W, d) 33.3%

10  a) 1680 MJ, b) 47.6%

11  a) $6.75 \times 10^5$ J; b) $5.4 \times 10^5$ J

12  a) 20 W, b) 21 600 J

13  When 1 kg of coal is burned it produces 30 MJ
    of heat energy. However, as the coal burns,
    the energy is degraded as the 30 MJ cannot all
    be changed into electrical energy due to some
    of the heat energy being lost to the
    surroundings.

14  a) Fission, b) neutrons, c) A chain reaction
    occurs when each fission produces at least one
    further fission.

## 6.3   SOURCE TO CONSUMER

1   a) Diagrams A, C and E, b) stronger magnet;
    more turns of wire on coil; coils moved faster
    through magnetic field.

2   P = Iron casing, Q = Stator, R = Dynamo
    (exciter), S = Rotor (field coils).

3   a) The pointer deflects to one side of the
    voltmeter, returns to zero, then deflects to the
    other side, returns to zero as the magnet
    makes each revolution.
    b) No moving parts to collect the large
    currents generated, c) Commercial generator
    is much bigger, produces a larger current and
    uses an electromagnet instead of a permanent
    magnet.

4   a) A transformer changes the magnitude (size)
    of an a.c. voltage.

b) Require wire and an iron core (e.g. iron
nail). Wind a number of turns of wire onto the
iron core. Then wind a second set of turns of
wire to produce two separate coils of wire
wrapped round the iron core.

5   a) 230 V, b) 4 V, c) 40 turns, d) 1350 turns

6   a) 8 V, b) 11.5 V, c) 24 V

7   a) 125 V, b) 230 V, c) 300 V

8   a) 30 turns, b) 40 turns, c) 60 turns

9   a) 40 turns, b) 1600 turns, c) 400 turns

10  a) 230 V, b) 6 V, c) 6 A, d) 1.2 A

11  a) 3 A, b) 8 A, c) 0.5 A

12  a) 0.25 A, b) 24 A, c) 0.5 A

13  Heat, sound, magnetic field lost from
    transformer.

14  To minimise the power lost (as heat) in the
    transmission lines.

15  A = step-up transformer, B = pylons,
    C = grid network, D = step-down
    transformer, E = homes, F = 25 000 V,
    G = 400 000 V, H = 230 V

16  a) 12 V, b) 2 A, c) 0.2 A

17  a) a.c., b) 200, c) 5 W, d) 5.75 W, e) 0.025 A

18  a) 1250 A, b) 25 Ω, c) 39 MW, d) 461 MW,
    e) 92.2%

19  a) 10 V, b) 1 A, c) 10 W

## 6.4   HEAT IN THE HOME

1   Temperature, Celsius, heat, conduction,
    convection, radiation

2   a) Convection, b) radiation, conduction

3   a) e.g. Double glazing reduces conduction
    from windows due to vacuum between
    windows. Wooden frames surrounding
    windows reduce conduction through the
    frames, b) e.g. Loft insulation reduces
    convection into the loft by trapping a layer of
    air; cavity wall insulation reduces convection
    in the cavity by trapping the air in the cavity

c) e.g. Putting a layer of silver foil behind a radiator reduces heat loss by radiation as the silver foil reflects the heat from the radiator back into the room; a layer of gold on windows allows heat radiation to pass from outside the house inside but reflects heat radiation from the room back.

4 Thursday

5 Copper, since specific heat capacity of copper is greater than the specific heat capacity of lead.

6 a) 16 720 J, b) 83 600 J, c) 75 240 J

7 a) 4000 J, b) 400 J/kg °C, c) 5 kg, d) 6°C

8 90 200 J

9 $1.672 \times 10^5$ J

10 a) 9750 J, b) 9020 J, c) 92.5%

11 133.76 s

12 2400 J/kg °C

13 a) $9.936 \times 10^6$ J, b) 26.3°C, c) Heat is 'lost' from the water.

14 Refrigerator, ice pack for a picnic box.

15 c m $\Delta$T, specific heat capacity, m l, fusion, vaporisation

16 a) 7500 J, b) 0.25 kg, c) 334 000 J/kg, d) 33 400 J, e) 904 000 J/kg

17 a) $3.34 \times 10^5$ J, b) $6.68 \times 10^5$ J, c) $1.67 \times 10^6$ J, d) $2.672 \times 10^5$ J

18 a) $2.26 \times 10^6$ J, b) $4.52 \times 10^6$ J, c) $1.13 \times 10^7$ J, d) $1.808 \times 10^6$ J

19 $2.2 \times 10^{-2}$ kg

20 a) 23 040 J, b) 0.02 kg

# Answers to Exam Style Questions

1 a) Chemical to kinetic to heat,
b) $3.96 \times 10^{12}$ J, c) 36.7%, d) radioactive waste

2 a) 4000 W, b) 8%, c) i) Clean, free, etc., ii) No energy produced in darkness, large number of panels required, etc.

3 a) i) 0.02 A, ii) 69 J, b) i) 2.7 J, ii) 3.9%

4 a) i) The pointer deflects to one side of the voltmeter, returns to zero, then deflects to the other side, returns to zero as the magnet moves in and out of the coil each time,
ii) Make magnet move faster; use a stronger magnet; have more turns on the coil,
b) i) 1.5 A, ii) A) 27.2 W B) 3.2 J, iii) sound is produced, heat is produced, magnetic field lost from the transformer.

5 a) 535.7 J/kg °C, b) Steel, c) i) e.g. Place a polystyrene sheet below block, ii) e.g. Wrap block in cotton wool, iii) e.g. Place silver foil round the block.

6 a) 228 s, b) Heat energy is transferred to the surroundings. This means the kettle has to supply the energy to change the temperature of the water and the energy for the surroundings. Since Energy = power × time then the kettle will be on for a longer time, c) 0.097 kg

# 7 Space Physics

## 7.1 DETECTING SIGNALS FROM SPACE

1 a) d = v × t = $3 \times 10^8 \times 60 = 1.8 \times 10^{10}$ m
b) d = $1.8 \times 10^{10} \times 24 \times 60$
= $2.59 \times 10^{13}$ m
c) $2.59 \times 10^{13} \times 365 = 9.5 \times 10^{15}$ m

2 d = $4.3 \times 9.5 \times 10^{15} = 4.085 \times 10^{16}$ m

3

| Term | Meaning |
|------|---------|
| **Planet** | An object that orbits a star |
| **Moon** | An object that orbits a planet |
| **Star** | A ball of gases that produces heat and light |
| **Galaxy** | A system of stars and dust that is spinning and travelling |
| **Universe** | The whole of space that can be detected |

**4** 100 000 years

**5**

Objective — Eyepiece

**6**

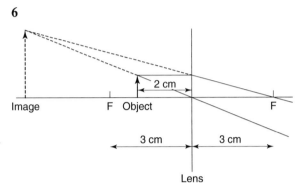

Image | F Object | F
2 cm
3 cm | 3 cm
Lens

b) The image is magnified, upright and cannot be caught on a screen.
c) 2.5

**7** A larger diameter of lens to collect more light.

**8** a) Red, green and blue. b) Red

**9** a) Radio, infra red, visible, ultraviolet, X-rays
b) $3 \times 10^8$ m/s

**10**

| Radiation | Detector |
|-----------|----------|
| Radio waves | **Aerial** |
| Infra red | **Photo transistor** |
| **Visible** | The eye |
| Ultraviolet | **Fluorescent material** |
| **X-rays** | Photographic film |
| **Gamma rays** | G-M tube |

**11** a) Aerial, b) The wavelengths are not in the visible range.

**12** a) b) 2

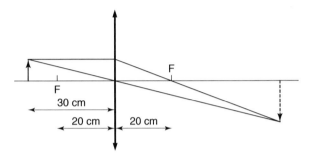

F
30 cm
20 cm | 20 cm

**13** a) b) 0.7

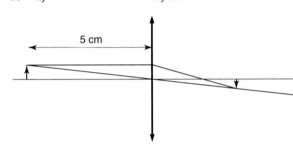

5 cm

**14** 10 cm

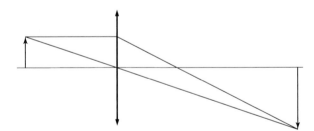

## 7.2 SPACE TRAVEL

**1**

Engine thrust

Weight

**2** a) $W = mg = 2 \times 10^6 \times 10 = 2 \times 10^7$ N
b) $2.1 \times 10^7 - 2 \times 10^7 = 1 \times 10^6$ N
c) $a = F/m = 1 \times 10^6/2 \times 10^6 = 0.5$ m/s$^2$

**3** a) 10 m/s$^2$ b) All objects if reasonably compact will fall at the same rate.
c) On Earth, hammer reaches ground first. On Mars, both will hit the ground at the same time.
d) On Earth there is air resistance. On Mars there is no air resistance.

**4**

| Planet | Gravitational field strength | Mass in kg | Weight in N |
|--------|------|------|------|
| Earth | 10 | 5 | **50** |
| Moon | 1.6 | 8 | **12.8** |
| Mars | **14** | 4 | 56 |
| Saturn | **8** | 11 | 88 |
| Jupiter | 26 | 5 | 130 |
| Venus | 9 | 8 | 72 |
| Mercury | 4 | 8 | 32 |

**5** a) 25 N b) i) Both fall at the same rate.
ii) Zero newtons

**6** Forces always act in pairs which are equal in size but opposite in direction.

**7** a) The force acting on unit mass.
b) Decreases.

**8** a) Height should increase. b) The satellite falls towards the Earth at the same rate as the Earth surface falls away.

**9** You appear to weigh eight times your weight on Earth.

**10** It heats up.

**11** a) The tiles withstand the repeated heating as the spacecraft enters the Earth's atmosphere.
b) The white tiles reflect the heat and keep the craft cool. The black tiles are used to withstand the high temperatures.

**12** a) $E_k = 1/2\, mv^2 = 1/2 \times 800 \times (850^2 - 150^2)$
$= 2.8 \times 10^8$ J
b) i) $2.8 \times 10^8$ J ii) $2.8 \times 10^8/(800 \times 1100)$
$= 318°C$.

**13** a) i)

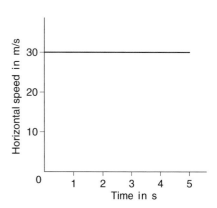

ii)

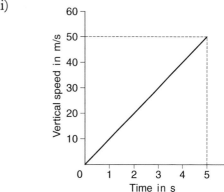

b) $d = V_H \times t = 30 \times 5 = 150$ m
c) Height = Area under $V_v - t$ graph
$= \frac{1}{2} \times 50 \times 5 = 125$ m

**14** a)

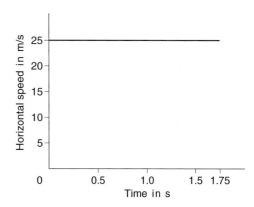

b) $v = u + at = 10 \times 1.75 = 17.5$ m/s
c) $17.5/2 = 8.75$ m/s
d) Height = Average speed $\times$ time
$= 8.75 \times 1.75$
$= 15.3$ m

## Answers to Exam Style Questions

1  a) $W = mg = 4 \times 10^6\,N$;
   Unbalanced force $= 1.6 \times 10^7 - 4 \times 10^6$
   $= 1.2 \times 10^7\,N$
   $a = F/m = 1.2 \times 10^7/4 \times 10^5 = 30\,m/s^2$
   b) If thrust is constant and $a = F/m$, a must increase
   c) $E_k = \frac{1}{2}mv^2$
   $= \frac{1}{2} \times 2800 \times (1200)^2$
   $= 2.016 \times 10^9\,J$
   d)             $E_k = E_h$
   $2.016 \times 10^9 = cm\,\Delta T$
   $= c \times 2800 \times 1100$
   $c = 655\,J/kg\,°C$

2  a) Distance travelled by light in one year.
   b) $1.71 \times 10^{17}\,m$, c) i) To collect the parallel rays of light and bring them to a focus. ii) To magnify the final image.

3  a) The chemicals that make up the star.
   b) This star is closer. c) More light would be detected.

4  a) The satellite will fall towards the Earth at the same rate as the surface of the Earth falls away.
   b) Decrease c) Increases d) Kinetic energy will change to heat and it may burn up.

5  a) 60 kg, b) 600 N, c) In the shuttle,
   d) Gravity is less on the moon and there is no air resistance.

6  a) Decreases b) It decreases c) The forces are now balanced.

# Data sheet

*Speed of light in materials*

| Material | Speed in m/s |
|---|---|
| Air | $3.0 \times 10^8$ |
| Carbon dioxide | $3.0 \times 10^8$ |
| Diamond | $1.2 \times 10^8$ |
| Glass | $2.0 \times 10^8$ |
| Glycerol | $2.1 \times 10^8$ |
| Water | $2.3 \times 10^8$ |

*Gravitational field strengths*

| | Gravitational field strength on the surface in N/kg |
|---|---|
| Earth | 10 |
| Jupiter | 26 |
| Mars | 4 |
| Mercury | 4 |
| Moon | 1.6 |
| Neptune | 12 |
| Saturn | 11 |
| Sun | 270 |
| Venus | 9 |

*Specific latent heat of fusion of materials*

| Material | Specific latent heat of fusion in J/kg |
|---|---|
| Alcohol | $0.99 \times 10^5$ |
| Aluminium | $3.95 \times 10^5$ |
| Carbon dioxide | $1.80 \times 10^5$ |
| Copper | $2.05 \times 10^5$ |
| Glycerol | $1.81 \times 10^5$ |
| Lead | $0.25 \times 10^5$ |
| Water | $3.34 \times 10^5$ |

*Specific latent heat of vaporisation of materials*

| Material | Specific latent heat of vaporisation in J/kg |
|---|---|
| Alcohol | $11.2 \times 10^5$ |
| Carbon dioxide | $3.77 \times 10^5$ |
| Glycerol | $8.30 \times 10^5$ |
| Turpentine | $2.90 \times 10^5$ |
| Water | $22.6 \times 10^5$ |

*Speed of sound in materials*

| Material | Speed in m/s |
|---|---|
| Aluminium | 5200 |
| Air | 340 |
| Bone | 4100 |
| Carbon dioxide | 270 |
| Glycerol | 1900 |
| Muscle | 1600 |
| Steel | 5200 |
| Tissue | 1500 |
| Water | 1500 |

*Specific heat capacity of materials*

| Material | Specific heat capacity in J/kg °C |
|---|---|
| Alcohol | 2350 |
| Aluminium | 902 |
| Copper | 386 |
| Diamond | 530 |
| Glass | 500 |
| Glycerol | 2400 |
| Ice | 2100 |
| Lead | 128 |
| Water | 4180 |

*Melting and boiling points of materials*

| Material | Melting point in °C | Boiling point in °C |
|---|---|---|
| Alcohol | −98 | 65 |
| Aluminium | 660 | 2470 |
| Copper | 1077 | 2567 |
| Glycerol | 18 | 290 |
| Lead | 328 | 1737 |
| Turpentine | −10 | 156 |

*SI prefixes and multiplication factors*

| Prefix | Symbol | Factor | |
|---|---|---|---|
| mega | M | 1 000 000 | $= 10^6$ |
| kilo | k | 1000 | $= 10^3$ |
| milli | m | 0.001 | $= 10^{-3}$ |
| micro | μ | 0.000 001 | $= 10^{-6}$ |

# Electrical and electronic graphical symbols

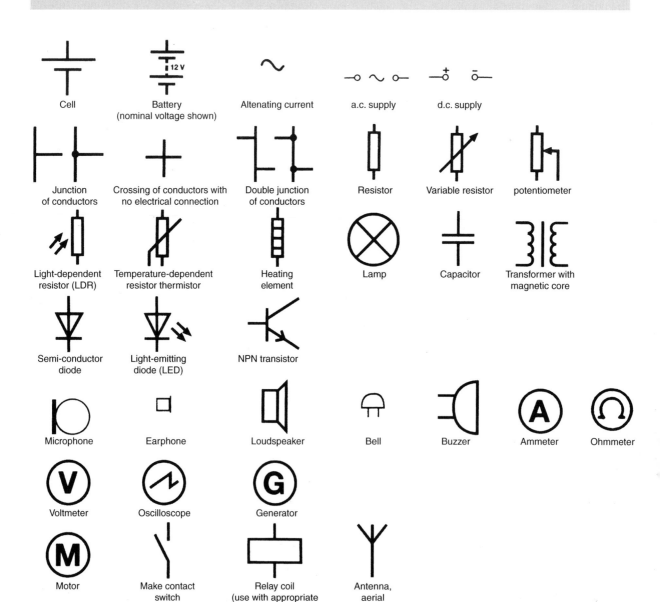

Cell

Battery
(nominal voltage shown)

12 V

Alternating current

a.c. supply

d.c. supply

Junction
of conductors

Crossing of conductors with
no electrical connection

Double junction
of conductors

Resistor

Variable resistor

potentiometer

Light-dependent
resistor (LDR)

Temperature-dependent
resistor thermistor

Heating
element

Lamp

Capacitor

Transformer with
magnetic core

Semi-conductor
diode

Light-emitting
diode (LED)

NPN transistor

Microphone

Earphone

Loudspeaker

Bell

Buzzer

Ammeter

Ohmmeter

Voltmeter

Oscilloscope

Generator

Motor

Make contact
switch

Relay coil
(use with appropriate
return switch)

Antenna,
aerial

Earth

Fuse

AND

OR

NOT (inverter)